APPALACHIAN HERITAGE

VOL. 45, NO. 4
FALL 2017

ESTABLISHED IN 1973

PUBLISHED QUARTERLY
by Berea College
CPO 2166
205 N. Main Street
Berea, KY, 40404

www.appalachianheritage.net

 Periodicals postage paid at Berea, Kentucky, and at additional mailing offices. ISSN# 03632318.

Electronic submissions only at www.appalachianheritage.net

Distributed by the University of North Carolina Press. Basic subscription price: $30/year for individuals, $40/year for institutions. For subscription requests and inquiries, visit the magazine's website, email uncpress_journals@unc.edu, or call 919.962.4201.

CONTENTS

POETRY

BOOK REVIEWS

COVER PHOTOGRAPH

Meg Wilson, *Creek Foxes*

SPECIAL ILLUSTRATIONS

Robert Gipe

EDITOR'S NOTE

JASON HOWARD

Seven years ago, I sat foot in Westminster Abbey for the first time. As a staunch Anglophile and lover of history, I was overwhelmed as I walked among the tombs and effigies and quire stalls, sensing the veil grow thin between present and past. But when I reached Poets' Corner—as I studied the memorials to Samuel Taylor Coleridge, A.E. Housman, and William Wordsworth—I was carried for a moment back across the ocean to Appalachia, back to a poet who numbers this trio among his literary heroes.

Since the publication of his debut collection, *Lawrence Booth's Book of Visions*, in 2001, Maurice Manning has established himself as one of America's preeminent poets of the rural, as his subsequent books have considered the life of Daniel Boone, the mysterious Creator of nature called Boss, the voices and stories of old-timers from deep Appalachian hollows, and the "dimming green" that underscores the gradual disappearance of rural life.

As this year's featured author, Manning has provided us with all new work—a clutch of startling poems that contemplates the joy, grief, and inherent mystery of rural life. The tellers of these poems call our attention to a truth "as plain / as a dead leaf": how nature can show us the way, how the history of a country can be buried in a rural place name, how art can be found in the feather of a humble bird. The power and poetic impulse behind such renderings are also on display, found both in Manning's craft essay about Wallace Stevens and in his interview with friend and fellow poet Marianne Worthington.

In this issue we are also proud to feature astonishing work from a number of talented writers, including Deborah Reed Downing, whose story "Fish and Wildlife" was recently awarded the Betty Gabehart Prize from the Kentucky Women Writers Conference; Jessie van Eerden, whose essay "Yoke" brims with rhythm and meaning; and Sean Patrick Hill, who takes us to the Red River Gorge in his essay "A Country of Edges"; and numerous others.

In "The Prelude," Wordsworth recalled his childhood, of being bequeathed A knowledge, a dim earnest, of the calm / That nature breathes among the hills and groves. May you encounter that wisdom in the gentle winds of these pages. ■

THE TALL BOOK

for Tony Earley and after his fashion

I've determined the quiet beauty of things
is what I hearken to, the grace
of a papery butterfly tipping
over the purple frill at the tops
of ironweed, the field splayed
up the hill and misty, the end of summer.
Nothing like an understatement
to inspire, or rain a flood in the mind
to leave it glimmering and deep.

—It's been a pretty good day. I've worked,
in the pastoral sense, under the sun,
and felt the heat, the idle shrug
of knowing the work is never done,
to make the world alive and living,
to make the mind's revealing vision

DREAMING MY WAY INTO SOMETHING
WHAT I HEARKEN TO
SOME
PLEASURE AFFEC-TION

tremble and shake itself alive,
as a butterfly wriggling out of
its sticky, round domain.

I can tell
I'm dreaming my way into something,
drifting along with the pleasant dream
and the voice of the dream telling it,
in a sonorous sound and rhythm I like.
Some of the words I used to hear
and say to myself over and over
have risen up. Playing by ear—
that's how I've always gone about it,
imagining the sound of a voice
and hearing in it, despite the clear
authority, some pleasure, affection.
Early on, I heard a lot
of wrong words, the garbled language,
and words put to inventive use.
I was often told to quiten down

in school. Or an old man would say
at night, it's quite alright, and stare
into a distance he seemed to see
the other side of, where Silence lived,
the sole ghost of another country.
And there were mystical tones and forms
I liked to hear—Quitchyomeddlin—
that sounded like the name of a man
who lived in a tall tale and drank
a pond of water every morning
and picked his teeth with a cedar tree,
or tamed a pair of rattlesnakes
to keep his britches histed up.
He was 27 feet tall
and played a fiddle made from a coffin.—

Histed up. Quitchyomeddlin—
what kind of bride would marry him?
I liked to make him real to me,
and follow him to the quitened place.

COULD HAVE BEEN
SAY@NIGHT IT'S QUITE ALL RIGHT.

WE AINT EAT NOBODY YET.
GROUND SO PUNY.

Sometimes thinking about a word
and the voice that said it moves me to tears.
A scalded dog. The Reachin' Pole.
The Wavingest Man that Ever Was.

It could have been that Quitchyomeddlin
and his woman had a pair of sons—
Ontellinmeddlin and Woesomemeddlin,
but called them Tell and Some for short.
They were a practical tribe, like Moses
or Noah, old testament folks,
who wandered wherever no one else
was at—so far up a holler they had
to pipe in sunlight, and the ground
was so puny they fertilized
the fenceposts to keep them stuck.

But Tell and Some were kindly shy,
and one day they said to Quitchyomeddlin,
—Pappy, we ain't hardly fit

to be in no tall tale! We're shy!
And we're pert near civilized,
and we ain't eat nobody yet,
nor swallered up the clouds, nor clomb
a vine to the yonder-side of heaven!
The father calmly raised a brow,
prompting his shavers, now, to think.

—Reckon I could gnaw on a leg
to see if I like eatin' people,
said Tell.

            —And they's a passel of vines
all over this territory, said Some,
I figure they's one worth climbin' up.

Quitchyomeddlin twisted his whiskers
around like a rag and pondered his chaps.

Aye gonnies, boys, you've got to wait!
They's a heap of time in a tall tale
that don't get counted for and passes
as quite as a river in the shade.
A feller has to sleep, and set
hisself on a stump and see what's what—
but then with a clap of thunder he's off
on something dramatical, and the clouds
go to making furrows in the sky
and pretty soon a witch shows up,
the tale comes back and follers on—
you pups'll have tall tales a-plenty—
Bangers, if you ain't in one now!
You might even find yourselves set down
one day on the leaves of the tall book,
right there aside of Old Jack.

As quite as a river in the shade—
I gave those words to Quitchyomeddlin,
and in my mind as he said them, he blew

DOTS TO MARK
GAVE THOSE WORDS 2 Q
THE QUIET SHE REQUIRED.

a tuft of whiskers out of his mouth.
I had him fashioned as a man
who'd let a wilderness grow on his face.
A man who couldn't read a lick,
and now he's got a tale of his own.
I like the rattlesnake suspenders.
I also like the river curled
like a snake asleep on a branch in the scene,
and the rhythm slinking through the words
in time with the silent, lazy river.
The symbols, the archetype, the stillness,
up there in the misty, hazy hills,
with the river wandering below.

—Miss Hazel Moseley—that was her name,
the teacher who told me to quiten down.
She had to say it many times.
I remember her heavy black shoes
and the clod-hopping sound she made
clomping across the room—dots

bewildering
DELIGHT.

to mark the quiet she required.
She was short, below five feet,
and as stout as a brimming coffee pot.

You have to keep the language alive—
that's something I've learned from listening.
I've also learned from watching the world,
a butterfly completely yellow,
a pale yellow the color of butter,
and the butterfly bending over
the purple top of ironweed
in a shaggy field on the side of a hill,
the beauty of what is and the words for it.
I find it all bewildering
and filled with love, a voice hearing
itself caught in a moment of grace
or a moment of quiet delight, delight.

MAURICE MANNING

THE TRUTH ON THREE LICK CREEK

Below the ridges, dim and low,
the hollows and narrow valleys run,
and pools of water prove a stream
has been there once. Standing before
a pool like these, painted with leaves
dropped from the trees, I now believe
a mind conceived this place and thought,
it must be sunken down, and save
the birds and wind and other sounds
belonging to it, it must be quiet.
And let the truth of this be as plain
as a dead leaf, the mind has said.
We'll bring a boy down here one day
and see if he can handle it.

MAURICE MANNING

LITTLE GREY FEATHER TINGED WITH RED OR BLOOD

I don't know what to think, standing
at the bottom of the hill in the woods.
The bare trees reach up. The hill
is to my right and on the left
begins another, steeper hill.
We call this a hollow, as if this place
were empty. I like such irony—
it won't explain itself, and here
is nothing explicable. We make
comparisons to it, but not
the other way around, except
to say, the foot of the hill, the head
of the hollow. Usually we say,
a man has cavernous eyes, so the eyes
mean more, and the man himself becomes
more fundamentally defined.
Someone could come here and learn nothing.
I was raised to think God was involved with this—
no, I wasn't raised that way;
it was my idea all along,
I found it all by myself, standing
in the woods when I was a boy, merely
a boy looking up at the trees,
or down at a feather dropped in the grass,
a feather representing both
itself and the bird, and even more
at once, as if it were an art.

MAURICE MANNING

PEOPLE OF SENSIBILITY

People of sensibility
like to admire a painting or some
possession, but a different mind
will linger over the bluish feather
sticking out of the shot glass
someone set on the windowsill
austerely, or even the little chip
of a plate found in the flower bed,
or watching someone fall asleep.
Most time goes by this way, with something
seemingly trivial happening.
Who broke the plate? That's one question.
Who threw it in the flower bed?
Who is that sleeping with the book
half cradled in her hands? Who brought
the chip from the plate back in the house?
No telling what kind of book she's reading,
but the title has an L in it
between her fingers on the spine,
a capital L is sitting there
importantly. The feather has also
made an impression, but the decision
to leave it barely noticeable,
not centered in the window but
at the edge, is the sort of thing someone
would say is beautiful.

MAURICE MANNING

READING A BOOK IN THE WOODS

The spindly trunks of two trees
have twisted twice around each other.
This is what I see when I look up
from reading. I've read the page on the right
then turned to the left-hand page and read.
I've read the book all out of order,
beginning in the middle. Now,
by looking up, I know the book
is reading me. And there I am
in a middle chapter, whistling,
and knocking the back of my hand against
the motionless fruits of a hawthorn tree,
an action that has no consequence
unless the lifted hand and the branch
left swaying after are symbolic.
I could see it that way, but also see
how simple it is, how very little
is happening—no memory
is leaking out, no evident
signs of despair. There's sort of a dot,
dot, dot at this point in the book,
and I don't think the ending offers
much more. Maybe the sun goes down
and someone whistles in the dark,
or maybe it ends with pale light
still visible above the trees
and one has been changed, and walks farther
into the woods and farther than that.

MAURICE MANNING

LOVE POEM

for Amanda

The dry vine from a kind of weed
whose yield is pods is being flung
out senselessly by the wind, and a scrap
of the vine at that, the part still curled
around the cedar branch, its host,
with a kite-tail hanging down,
and one of the pods is open like
a heart on a paper Valentine
from school I used to get and used
to make by folding the paper in half
and turning it around the scissors,
mostly for friendship, or to do
what everybody else would do,
but the hearts I made were always off.
This one, fluttering from the vine
that's fastened to the branch of the tree,
was full of seeds that floated away
in the fall, then winter happened to it.
And there it is, just hanging there,
as if someone tied it to the branch
and the vine had no decision in it.

MAURICE MANNING

THE WAY

Hindman, Kentucky, November 18, 2012

Standing beside the tree invites
belief, my spirit or soul answers
an easy or crazy waving leaf,
or even a motionless leaf, even
in winter the stark unmoving branch—
or from a distance the tree itself.
But after belief the preachers I heard
when I was younger never said
what happens then. Just go along
and be alive? It's hard to live that way,
for me it is. I remember seeing,
The Way, in bright lettering
on a book, and hearing about the path,
and wondering where we are going and when
will we start and could I bring the dog.
That was forty years ago
when I traced my fingers over the letters,
and sometime after that I knew,
how people suffer and grieve and sit there,
like a piece of wire stuck to a post.

MAURICE MANNING

SUBLIMITY

It has been experienced many times that mountain people live where they do because that is where and how they prefer to live.

—A History of the Daniel Boone National Forest
1770-1970, *U.S. Forest Service*

Somewhere along the way to being
must also be belonging, because
being is not an isolation
or even some distinction, but
to be a part, and a part becomes
distinct by being home, provided
home is the land, varied, changing,
oblivious to anything
but becoming its expression, like
a voice capable of song
and silence that even silent gives
what is vaguely, hopefully called
a presence, at times unnamable.
Walk up a hill sometime and see
in the valley a few barns, what must
be houses, a country store, a church
or a school, some sheep in a field below
a lower hill on the farther side.
I'm thinking of a place like Mossy
or Level Green, two villages
I've seen below, so named for what
they are. To see them there, not far,
though from a distance that clarifies
and also makes a kind of dream—
I've needed the hill; and needed my mind,

my being, to become the hill,
to be of the hill as a tree is of it,
or a shadow falling over it,
a thing inside the everything,
where it is possible to live
at Level Green or Mossy, but
the real belonging is to the hill.
Even now thinking about the hill,
imagining perspective, I'm lost
because I'm there—and my being there
is being there when I am not.

MAURICE MANNING

CHICKEN BRISTLE

There's a place near here called Chicken Bristle.
It's not a very hopeful name,
but it's out in the country and quiet. A handful
of houses are clustered along a lane.
The land is rolling and secret and dark.
My grandmother lived there when she was a girl,
but then it was known as Turnersville—
if you were white. If you were black,
you lived in Chicken Bristle, Kentucky.
I've seen a map that says the place
is Turnersville, but then a pair
of parentheses has Chicken Bristle
between the crescent moon-like curves.
The curves are like unspoken verses,
and Chicken Bristle is more than a name.
I don't think anyone, black or white,
prospered there. It was just a place
to live and long and love your people.
It wasn't a place for prospering,
and, anyway, enriching yourself
with simple riches isn't really
prosperity. It's better to know
the land around you is rolling and dark,
pastoral and lulling, and hard.
You set your mind and body to work
and hope the work will reach your heart,
to see, in that repose, some beauty,
some meaning for a human life.
And there you have it, America,
your history in brief. I think
you need to live and long, and love

your people. I'm writing this poem while
my daughter sleeps in quiet peace,
only the sound of my pen scratching
its marks on the page, her whistling breath.
It's late in the night. One of these days
I'm going to take her to Chicken Bristle
and hold her up to the air and the wild
and say to her, part of you, my love,
comes from Chicken Bristle, this dark
and lulling place, sprung up like
a thistle-patch among the hills.
But isn't it beautiful? Isn't
there sweetness in the very air?

MAURICE MANNING

AN IRON RING FASTENED TO A RAIL IN THE BARN

I've got a banjo six feet long
and a red-handled Barlow knife,
so I've got the credentials, Mister, to do
the things I do. It takes a lot
of figuring and time to do it.
The barn is just an empty church,
a solemn spirit is inside it.
Something was tied to a rail, because
an iron ring is fastened there—
maybe to suffer, I don't know.
A world of art is in front of you,
not always elegant art, but art
that reveals its passion. I've decided
to love the elegant less than I love
the wild, the untamed passionate art.
The blurt and cackle of birds, the look
of a curled-up lower leaf on a tree,
the tree itself from underneath—
the unexpected shadowy shape.
This distance across the hills is something
you can hear, like a voice. It's space and time
and the sky-domed air and objects and trees,
the shapes of living things, the wonder
of everything, the only art.
Even a world that's surreal begins
with the world as it is in plain sight
and mystical for being itself.
And what am I to do, to add
to it my little portion of being?
Whoever heard of a six-foot banjo?

That's like playing a man—but playing a man
or a longish woman is something you have
to do if you're serious about
this art, and I don't mean poetry,
I mean the larger art of being
alive in the world and suddenly seeing
an iron ring and wondering what
was its use and if it was an art
and if there was suffering involved.
I've come to believe that art can be
a beautiful, necessary wound,
a piercing of the soul and then,
after a dark time, a joy.

MAURICE MANNING

WHY I AM NOT A STOIC

By now I've seen it all, the weird
translucent yellow spider hauling
her pale pearl of eggs, or the spores
of the reddish fungus fuming out
from its half-inch smokestack
in the moss, and even the damp shade
commencing with the woods and seeming
like water steadily to flow
away—how these go unattended—
an observation so smug and pithy
I ought to take it back, but I mean it
as a fact, as a starting point, in case
a philosophical moment arrives.
It would suit me if it didn't, because
a philosophy based on shade or moss
would be difficult to prove. I've made
a claim—the appearance of something that seems
singular, but probably isn't,
and that an irony observed
in what I thought was solitude.
But I was never alone in the shade—
I had the shade and the moss inside it,
and the poof of spores, and the yellow spider
swinging back and forth like a bulb
in a room with someone listening
to nothing or a bug flicking
against the black pane of the window.
We have a form inside a form
inside a mesmerizing form.
I'm itching to say something nice
about it—it's pleasantly slow, and may

appeal to objectivity—
but maybe not. Let's let it be
night-time now up there in the dome
of contemplation, no light, no need
to have a light. Let's give it a rest,
let's say, Good-night, you little idea.

MAURICE MANNING

WALLACE STEVENS: HILLBILLY DELUXE

MAURICE MANNING

Twenty years ago, I was cavorting around the Kentucky backroads one day and happened upon the village of Mackville. While there I briefly visited with a lady, Mrs. Leonard Carpenter, the proprietress of the general store, who was in a guff because she'd moments before shooed away an idle youth—whom she referred to as a "nosey peckerwood"—from the shed behind her store. She allowed he was the eldest offspring of a whole family of idlers and little could be expected of the young man's future. "You just can't get above your raisin'," dame Carpenter said. Raisin' and rearin' up happen to be an interest of mine concerning Wallace Stevens: his poems strike us as the work of a seasoned and urbane man; it is surprising to think he had a childhood, and perhaps more surprising to learn that late in life he "dealt" with his childhood, as so many poets do, yet, characteristic of Stevens, his dealing was consciously impersonal and vague.

I've been looking through Stevens's letters, journals and some of the endnotes to the Library of America edition of his poetry and prose. Among the happier discoveries I've made rooting around in Stevens's life is the fact that his father was once the owner of a bicycle factory. In the summer of 1895 Stevens provided one fourth of a barbershop quartet, singing, not surprisingly, bass. As a law student in New York, Stevens took to walking around the city and its then outskirts; on one excursion he covered forty-one miles—in a single day! In 1936 at the age of fifty-five, clearly in possession of more than a petal from the flower of his youth, Stevens broke his hand in two places, after landing a punch on the jaw of one Ernest Hemingway, at some kind of artsy frat-party in Key West. Less happy is the fact that Stevens's parents—for reasons I haven't been able to unearth—disapproved of his marriage to Elsie Moll in September of 1909; in fact, they refused to attend the wedding. Stevens's father, Garrett, died two years later following a series of breakdowns; after the wedding, Stevens never spoke to his father again. Stevens's mother, Kate, died a year after her husband. I feel certain the family rift also severed Stevens's emotional connection to his hometown of Reading, Pennsylvania, and the surrounding hinterlands, and this break caused him grief, which would show up many years later "worked out," so to speak, in some of his driest, heady poems.

This rift and, particularly, the way it manifests itself in Stevens's poetry is the source of the criticism Randall Jarrell levels at Stevens. Jarrell says:

> *As a poet Stevens has every gift but the dramatic. It is the lack of immediate contact with lives that hurts his poetry more than anything else, that has made it easier and easier for him to abstract, to philosophize, to treat the living dog that wags its tail and bites you as the 'canoid patch' of the epistemologist analyzing that great problem, the world; as the 'cylindrical arrangement of brown and white' of the aesthetician analyzing that great painting, the world.*[1]

Jarrell's assessment is one with which I would politely disagree. If poetry, as Wordsworth claims, "is the spontaneous overflow of powerful feelings... recollected in tranquility," perhaps, then in the case of Stevens, it simply takes longer for the feeling to reach its full power, and further, perhaps recollection in Stevens requires several stages of reflection, so that the emotion—and implicit drama—which eventually finds its way to the page cooks the spontaneity down to a distilled and aged dram—the original sour mash has matured.[2] In short, Wordsworth is advocating moonshine; Stevens gives us mellow, eight-year-old bourbon. My notion is the powerful feeling and the drama are there, but filtered through several removes which merely create a different kind of poem. Stevens's letters and journals are the best means I've found to support my claim to the presence of real people and real drama, and if you don't mind I'd like to share a few excerpts with you. They've been a lot of fun to read and ponder.

It might shock some Modernist purists, but I think Stevens discusses his childhood, the small-town and rural world he knew, in profoundly Romantic terms, that is, as Wordsworth would recall his own childhood, as the source of the generative imagination, primed and pumped by adventures in the natural world. Here is Stevens writing in his journal during his first summer break from law school. He has returned to the Reading area.

> *The first day of one's life in the country is generally a day of wild enthusiasm. Freedom, beauty, sense of power etc.... [which leads to] the growth of small, specific observation. Weary of the deep horizon or green hills one finds immense satisfaction in studying the lyrics of song-sparrows, catbirds, wrens and the like. A valley choked with corn assumes a newer and more potent interest when one comes to notice the blade-like wind among the leaves; the same is true of flowers and birds in big grain-fields, of birds in the air, dashing toward the splendid clouds with a carol of joy, then suddenly wheeling and circling back to the clover and timothy in the most graceful of beauty lines. Orchards are enriched by the thought that they were almost prismatic in May; and by the sound of the rain upon their invisible leaves at midnight.*[3]

That could have come from *The Prelude*!

1 Randall Jarrell. "Reflections on Wallace Stevens." *Wallace Stevens: The Critical Heritage*, Charles Doyle, Ed. (New York: Routledge, Kegan and Paul, 1986), 334.

2 William Wordsworth. "Preface." *Lyrical Ballads: 1798 and 1802*, William Wordsworth and Samuel Taylor Coleridge. (Oxford: Oxford University Press, 2013), 98.

3 Journal recorded in Berkeley, Pennsylvania, 26 July 1899, during summer holiday.

It was on a similar visit home a few years later that Stevens met Elsie Moll and fell in love. Some of Stevens's earliest aesthetic principles and musings are spelled out in letters to Elsie. He also allows himself to be self-revealing and conventionally passionate. Here is Stevens's response to a letter from Elsie in which she obviously asked him to speak about his early childhood in Reading.

> *Secret* memoires: *go back to the bicycle period, for example—and before that to the age of the velocipede. Yes: I had a red velocipede that broke in half once going over a gutter in front of Butcher Deems (where the fruit store is now, beyond the Auditorium)—and I hurt my back and stayed away from school.—On Sundays, in those days, I used to wear patent leather pumps with silver buckles on 'em—and go to Sunday school and listen to old Mrs. Keeley, who had wept with joy over every pap in the Bible.—It seems now that the First Presbyterian church was very important: oyster suppers, picnics, festivals. I used to like to sit back of the organ and watch the pump-handle go up and down.... And I had a pirate period somewhere. I used to 'hop' coal-trains and ride up the Lebanon Valley and stone farm-houses and steal pumpkins and so on—with a really rough crowd.*[4]

In another letter to Elsie, Stevens distinguishes the outskirts of New York in 1909 from the countryside around Reading.

> *The country here is simply a place where there aren't many houses.... There's one fundamental difference that has nothing to do with the difference in the country itself. I am not emotional; but I am aware that I look at*

the country at home with emotion. The twenty years of life that are the simplest and the best were spent there [Reading]. It has become a memorable scene. But I do not look at the country here with emotion. When it is beautiful I know that it is beautiful. When the country at home is beautiful, I don't only know it; I feel it—I rejoice in it, and I am proud.[5]

Yet, not surprisingly—and I think this happens to many poets—Stevens's relationship to his homeland was not to stay so simple. As far as I can tell, there is no available record of whatever argument Stevens might have had with his parents over his marriage to Elsie. There are indications that her family wasn't too pleased either. The situation must have been very unpleasant, and no doubt cast a shadow over the marriage. The family rift had one practical effect on Stevens:

This sort of social independence...reinforces Stevens's poetic independence, and encourages his lifelong fascination with the force of the individual imagination...

he became increasingly independent, increasingly concerned with establishing his long-term professional and financial stability; he would be beholden to no one. This sort of social independence carries over, I think, and reinforces Stevens's poetic independence, and encourages his lifelong fascination with the force of the individual imagination, the allure of a privately constructed reality.

4 Letter to Elsie from New York recalling his childhood in Reading, 21 January 1909.

5 Letter to Elsie from New York, 13 July 1909.

Here, after his marriage, Stevens returns to Reading to visit his mother, Kate, who is near death. This is from the journal.

> *About a year ago (July 14, 1911) my father died. And now my mother is dying.... In the bed she is in now all of her children, except the first (and possibly him) were born. And there are a thousand things like that in the old house—certain chairs, certain closets, the side-board in the dining-room, her old piano (she would play hymns on Sunday evenings, and sing, I remember her studious touch at the piano, out of practice, and her absorbed, detached way of singing). At one period, say twenty years ago, she made efforts to get new things and many such objects remain: things in the parlor, etc. Her way of keeping things, or arranging rugs, of placing pieces of furniture, remains unaltered. A chair is where it is because she put it there and kept it there. The house is a huge volume full of the story of her thirty-five years or more within it.*[6]

This scene or an imagined, prior scene like it—or some fusion of those two kinds of reality—would haunt Stevens for thirty years. The bed in which he was born is the bed in which his mother will die. Although he has "broken" from this world, has he fully escaped it? Certainly an enduring closeness for his mother stayed with Stevens well after her death. But as I say, it took thirty years before this feeling—refined to a tincture—trickled out in the poems. His letters of the mid-1940s show a sudden willingness to think upon his early past, his ancestry. In 1942, Stevens contacts a couple of genealogists and puts them to work. Here are sections from various letters over a three-year period; note how Stevens opens up.

Mr. Lee has sent me word that you are trying to find out something about John Zeller, my mother's father. He used to live on Walnut Street, near Fourth, on the north side of the street. The house is still standing, but, beyond that and the strong chance that he was very much interested in the German Lutheran Church in the next block... I don't know a thing in the world about him.... We used to have at home two portraits, one of John Zeller, the man in whom I am interested, and another of his wife. I think that these were oils, but they might have been almost anything; they were certainly very depressing.[7]

My mother's father, John Zeller, was born in Berks County on October 21, 1809 and died at Reading on February 17, 1862.... He died, I believe, as a result of blood poisoning. My mother told me that he was fixing a fence and, somehow or other, cut himself with a nail. My grandfather was not born in Reading... but in Berks County. If he was born in Berks County, it is likely that he was the son of a farmer....The point of all this is that John was a country boy who must have spoken Pennsylvania Dutch. My mother spoke Pennsylvania Dutch, rather imperfectly, but always when she went to market and talked with the farmers' wives.[8]

I am a former resident of Reading. My mother was a member of the Zeller family. I am told that there are records of the family in your church papers and also that

6 Journal entry from 25 June 1912.

7 Letter 432 to Mary Owen Steinmetz, a genealogist working in Reading, Pennsylvania, 16 January 1942.

8 Letter 450 to Mary Owen Steinmetz, a genealogist working in Reading, Pennsylvania, 21 August 1942.

John Zeller, my great grandfather, who died about 1858, and his wife, who died some years later, are buried in the cemetery attached to the church. I should like very much to find out what the church records contain and have copies of any inscriptions on Zeller stones in the cemetery. John Zeller, my great grandfather, was a son of Francis, or Franz, Zeller. Franz lived in the Tulpehocken and he and his family were members of Trinity Tulpehocken Church.... The Zeller family seems to have been both poor and pious.[9]

The [Zeller?] family picture is like a good many other pictures of a different sort. There seems to be a tremendous thickness of varnish of a more or less romantic sort all over the thing, and I want to take that all off and get down to the real people. Several members of the family who have devoted themselves to the subject have gone in strongly for coats of arms and ancestral philosophers and scholars. I don't mean to say that I should be offended at the idea of being descended from Catharine de Medici, disreputable as she was, or any other Valois, disreputable as they were. But after muddling round with American genealogy for several years, I think that a decent sort of carpenter, or a really robust blacksmith, or a woman capable of having eleven sons and of weaving their clothes and the blankets under which they slept, and so on, is certainly no less thrilling.[10]

During this same period Stevens was working on *Transport to Summer*, his fifth book of poetry, published in 1947. As far as I can surmise, a good number of the poems in this book respond directly, if sometimes obliquely, to the landscape and atmosphere of Stevens's childhood in Reading and Bucks

County, and nearby Berks County, where Stevens often visited relatives. Among these "Pennsylvania Childhood Poems" are: "God is Good. It Is a Beautiful Night," "Dutch Graves in Bucks County, " "The Lack of Repose," "The Bed of Old John Zeller," "Wild Ducks, People and Distances," "Debris of Life and Mind," "Analysis of a Theme," "Late Hymn from the Myrrh-Mountain," "Pieces," "A Completely New Set of Objects," "Two Versions of the Same Poem," "Thinking of a Relation Between The Images of Metaphors," "Continual Conversation with a Silent Man," "Extraordinary References," "Credences of Summer," and sections of "Notes Toward a Supreme Fiction"—in short, a considerable portion of the book. Some of these poems clearly meditate on the beauty and ethos of a childhood that now—fifty years later—seems sadly remote and limited. Here's a stanza from "Dutch Graves in Bucks County:"

Who are the mossy cronies muttering,
Monsters antique and haggard with past thought?
What is this crackling of voices in the mind,
This pitter-patter of archaic freedom,
Of the thousands of freedoms except our own?

And you, my semblables, whose ecstasy
Was the glory of heaven in the wilderness—[11]

Here, Stevens sees how basically good intentions fall short, how the nobility of a particular vision—something to do with an American promise, I suspect—tarnishes once the limits of

9 Letter 511 to Dr. Howard Althouse, a minister, 9 August 1944.

10 Letter 545 to W.N.P. Daily, apparently a minister in the Reading region, 16 May 1945.

11 Stevens, *The Collected Poems* (New York: Vintage, 1990), 292.

that vision are discovered. And here we get a meditation on landscape, in "Extraordinary References:"

The cool sun of the Tulpehocken[12] *refers*
To its barbed, barbarous rising and has peace.
These earlier dissipations of the blood

And brain, as the extraordinary references
Of ordinary people, places, things,
Compose us in a kind of eulogy.[13]

And further landscape, this time from Berks County in "Credences of Summer:"

One of the limits of reality
Presents itself in Oley [a town] when the hay,
Baked through long days, is piled in mows. It is
A land too ripe for enigmas, too serene.[14]

Other poems in the set I've listed mention local towns, streams, and rivers, clearly remembered and recalled. Yet, to the casual reader, Stevens's references to people and places, while idiosyncratic in their way, often seem random, and often intentionally so. It's true, in other poems we see Stevens clearly drawn to stock characters, stock settings, a set of generic materials to demonstrate how the imaginative mind trumps any material reality. *The Collected Poems of Wallace Stevens,* assembled with his blessing just before he died in 1955, contains no footnotes; even the admirable Library of America edition provides few and brief notes, which help the poems to retain an air of secrecy. Perhaps wanting to know a few secrets, a few clues to what really burned in Stevens's prodigious belly, prompted my interest in these "Pennsylvania Childhood

Poems," the journals, and the letters. But it's often the case with Stevens, if you have a hint, the tiniest morsel of the real to which the artifice of the poem is a response, one stands a better chance of "getting" the poem, and really getting into it as well. That's the case with "The Bed of Old John Zeller," a kind of sad and funny poem, one in which the poet acknowledges his roots; acknowledges a kind of contempt for provincialism coupled with the ironic realization that he hasn't quite gotten above his raising despite achieving some objectivity; and most elegantly, arrives at a point of reconciliation, an understanding that the objective self the poet so ardently fussed over, nevertheless has humble, subjective beginnings. And perhaps that's not so bad. Here are a few passages from the poem—which is written in hexameters—and beg you to listen to bits and pieces of the letters and journals as they bubble to the surface.

This structure of ideas, these ghostly sequences
Of the mind, result only in disaster. It follows,
Casual poet, that to add your own disorder to disaster

Makes more of it. It is easy to wish for another structure
Of ideas and to say as usual that there must be
Other ghostly sequences and, it would be, luminous

Sequences, thought of among spheres in the old peak of
night:
This is the habit of wishing, as if one's grandfather lay
In one's heart and wished as he had always wished, unable
To sleep in that bed for its disorder, talking of ghostly

12 A region in Bucks County settled by Dutch Lutherans, his mother's family.
13 Stevens, *Collected Poems*, 369.
14 Ibid., 374.

Sequences that would be sleep and ting-tang tossing, so
that
He might slowly forget. It is more difficult to evade

That habit of wishing and to accept the structure
Of things as the structure of ideas. It was the structure
Of things at least that was thought of in the old peak of
night.[15]

And there we have it: the actual thing, the bed, considered as an abstraction; but then we realize Stevens is actually imagining an actual thing, so, on the other hand, he's pulled the abstraction back toward a kind of actual reality. Further, we have an imagined memory, since Stevens did not know Old John Zeller. It seems the impetus for the poem is the poet's desire to make an imagined past more real, and to demonstrate that process of imagining memory on the page. Along the way, however, I think Stevens realizes he cannot simplify the past, he cannot reduce it to stock symbols and hayseed characters. We're inclined to think the past, one's ancestry, ought to be logical—like the chain of "begats" in the Bible. A genealogical chart has a structure and an orderliness to it, full of straight lines. But such charts don't really explain anything beyond names and dates; they cannot possibly explain why Stevens would be haunted by a grandfather he never knew, or how the poet could imagine the grandfather, a dying patriarch riddled with regret, and feel with pleasure that he'd recalled and recreated a kindred spirit. ■

15 Ibid., 326.

AN *APPALACHIAN HERITAGE* INTERVIEW

MAURICE MANNING

Maurice Manning lives both in and apart from the world. On one hand, he is actively engaged with his own farm and is a vocal environmentalist and activist. He is a respected writer and teacher in local, regional, and national writing communities. On the other hand, he eschews any type of social media and can only bear to look at the news "just long enough to know what is going on." As a poet he is passionate about using language as a way to articulate and assign meaning to experiences, and yet he often isolates himself from worldly concerns while writing. Even his office on the busy campus of Transylvania University in Lexington, Kentucky, is located in a small tract house that sits on the edge of campus, away from the main buildings and gathering spots of campus life.

Manning's first book of poems, *Lawrence Booth's Book of Visions* (2001), was chosen by W.S. Merwin for the Yale Series of Younger Poets Award. His other collections are *A Companion for Owls: Being the Commonplace Book of D. Boone, Lone Hunter, Back Woodsman, & c.* (2004), *Bucolics* (2007), *The Common Man* (2010)—a finalist for the 2011 Pulitzer Prize—and *The Gone and the Going Away* (2013). In late 2016, his sixth collection of poems, *One Man's Dark*, was published by Copper Canyon Press.

Manning serves as professor of English and Writer-in-Residence at Transylvania and lives with his wife and daughter on twenty wooded acres in a 165-year-old farmhouse in Washington County, Kentucky, about fifteen miles from the city of Danville, Kentucky, where he was raised. A Guggenheim Fellow, Pulitzer finalist, and winner of many other prizes and fellowships, Manning also teaches regularly in the Warren Wilson MFA Program for Writers and at the annual Sewanee Writers' Conference.

He talked with his friend and fellow poet Marianne Worthington in that Transylvania office on a sunny afternoon in mid-September about his latest book of poems, the importance of craft in poetry, and the role of the artist in society.

■ ■ ■

photo: Steve Cody

Maurice Manning

MARIANNE WORTHINGTON: *One Man's Dark* has been summarized as "elegant pastorals" that combine the "corporeal and the spiritual." Likewise, another critic said the collection "emphasizes human beings' dependence on both nature and the divine, and thus the book is filled with poignant descriptions of nature's beauty... as well as with explicit references to God..." Were these ideas what you had in mind while you were writing the poems?

MAURICE MANNING: When I was working on the poems, my thinking was to work from a recurrent set of images. All of that was intentional on my part, and there's a motion to that because it is repetitive. And the writing style of this book is dense and repetitive in a way that a blackberry bramble is dense and stuck together. Or, in our region of the country when you look out at the hills, it's hard to tell when one hill ends and another begins. That sense of inter-connection, of inter-weaving, there's a motion and flow to that as well; there's a continuity in the landscape. I feel like this book is attempting to get hold of that, and I wanted the writing to parallel that.

MW: And what about the notion of the dream motif that also recurs throughout *One Man's Dark*?

MM: Actually, I would find myself writing many of the poems in my sleep. It's been rare when I've had an experience like that.

MW: Could you remember the poems when you woke up?

MM: Yes. I could remember lines. I could remember images. Certainly rhythms. And there was a point where, in the several years that I was working on the poems, it didn't matter to me to make a distinction between reality, memory, or dream. They all seemed to be flowing in and out of each other in a way that parallels what I was just saying about the landscape and the whole process of nature. We might be able to experience nature in its small parts but that's not what nature is. Nature is all of it, all at once, all the time. Usually for the purposes of some kind of art, we take a part of nature and focus on that. A poem of any kind isn't going to grab hold of it all. I was trying to at least imply the challenge of confronting the whole of nature and that it's the kind of challenge that makes you erase distinctions between memory, reality, and dream, to erase distinctions between the present and past. There's an effort to find the language to describe that kind of picture. My interest in that was most explicit. I was conscious of the effort.

MW: Could you talk about what the reviewers found in your poems that they've labeled as religious or spiritual dimensions?

MM: My only foundation was going to church every Sunday morning—an experience I had growing up. That just introduced the terms available for me to talk about spiritual encounter, but that doesn't bother me at all. I'm perfectly happy to use the terms of conventional religion in poetry. I was thinking about this last night. I had a moment, and I was working on a poem. The poem was about wondering whether or not God has stopped bothering with the world. Whatever intervention God may have done in the past, according to our scriptures, well maybe God is done with that. What do we do then? I was thinking what if God has checked out? Our attention seems to be so claimed by other things these days that God's response is to say, *Alright, then, let's see how you do.* I'm not trying to be funny about this; it was a serious

***The Gone and the Going Away* and *One Man's Dark* are Manning's most recent books.**

consideration. It's also the kind of thing that doesn't have an answer. You can't verify it. For me, that's what poetry does. It makes a connection between the thing that can possibly be witnessed or grasped or experienced and that thing that you see out in the world or beyond that is sort of the explanation or meaning of that experience. The poem for me is the means of going from one realm to the other, making that connection.

MW: Isn't that much like the definition of metaphor?

MM: It is. It is exactly, and that is why I think about metaphor all the time. It is a way to transfer significance from one domain to another, usually very different domains. And that is the practical value of a poem. And to go back to religious or spiritual matters, that's what prayer is for me. Prayer is in a similar category.

MW: Is the writing of a poem like a prayer for you?

MM: I had this very conversation the other day with a graduate student I'm working with. This is a matter that I've thought about a lot. I don't want to think that writing a poem is equivalent to prayer. I think that diminishes what prayer is and its purpose. I see the analogies between the two but I just don't want to get myself in the little box of saying, *oh, because I write poems I have a very rich and active prayer life.* And it's mainly because I want to realize the difference between the two and the different purposes of poetry and prayer. What I said to my student was: perhaps the poem that has a spiritual dimension to it is the effort the poet makes in *preparation* of prayer. Prayer would be a result of the poem, maybe, or a state of spiritual consciousness that the poem has made possible in some way. The prayer itself is beyond the poem or the writing of the poem. I'm still forming my thoughts about this, but some of my thinking is that poetry is too worldly, its concerns, its basis, and to me, prayer is willing to let go of worldliness. For instance, I enjoy going to the Abbey of Gethsemani near Bardstown, Kentucky, and just sitting in silence. I don't have to think about anything. In some ways, I'm emptying my thoughts in that place. My soul is restored in that kind of experience, and it is a wordless encounter and even a soundless encounter.

MW: Perhaps these thoughts are related to how the reviewer summarized your poems as "elegant pastorals" that combine the "corporeal and the spiritual"?

MM: In the summer of 2009 I went to Somerset County in southwestern England to the little village of Nether Stowey which is where Coleridge and Wordsworth met. That's where they took their famous walks, where they would walk all night long through the countryside or they'd walk forty miles a day and then they would write their now-famous poems. Coleridge's poems "This Lime-Tree Bower My Prison," "The Nightingale," and "Frost at Midnight" were written at this time. Wordsworth's poem "Tinturn Abbey" was written during that time, based on a walk he and Dorothy took a little farther north of Nether Stowey. Anyway, my goal was to take those Coleridge and Wordsworth poems and use them as a map. Then to walk, as best I could, the walk that the poems generated. It was amazing how possible that was to do. I had a topographic map, too, and I had put together enough background that I could kind of figure out the places on the earth that Coleridge was exactly describing in a poem. Syncing all that up was really a powerful experience for me. And it really inspired a lot of *One Man's Dark*. It clarified for me that it is possible to write directly about the landscape and that it is possible to trust that the landscape itself is generative of the poem. And that's what I realized Coleridge, especially, was doing—that the landscape corresponded to the mind and the undulations of the mind and all that fed the spirit. I realized I was trying to do that with the Kentucky landscape. And in particular a patch of the Kentucky landscape that is always in my mind. It's not just our farm in Washington County, although that is the center point, but it wanders down to Rockcastle and Pulaski Counties where my mother's people are from, on over to Clay County where my dad's people are from. It's an amalgamated landscape for me out of necessity but I wanted to prove to myself that the poems could come by being present in this specific landscape.

Most of the poems in *One Man's Dark* are in tetrameter, very much a walking meter, a purposeful and steady gait. That seemed suited to the scale of the landscape. That seemed suited to the idiom of our language around here. Very much a four-beat rhythm.

That's something I learned from Seamus Heaney, from studying his poems. There was some point in his career where he found the line. He found the vessel best suited for his expression and his sense of language and his idiomatic inheritance. And it was, I would say, a line that's flexible. It wasn't Elizabethan, iambic pentameter, it was missing a foot now and then, or had an extra foot now and then, and that flexibility allows so much in his poetry. I have since realized that instinctively I paid attention to that sort of thing in other poets. It was an epiphany in Heaney's work for me.

MW: Who are other poets who have influenced your work or other poets you are reading?

MM: R. S. Thomas, the Welsh minister, who does something similar to Heaney in that he is willing to be inconsistent (metrically) and not have all the edges polished. I go through phases, too, of recurring appreciations of different poets. I don't think I'll ever write a poem like Charles Wright or Brigit Pegeen Kelly or A. E. Stallings, but I enjoy studying their work. They are such gifted and agile poets. What I enjoy is how they use craft but also the idea of *what is the big claim here?* A poem can be topical, but what the poem is really saying can be way beyond its subject. I like that. You can see that the craft is what allows the poet to transcend the subject. Looking at the craft can get you to those deeper layers in a poem. It's like looking at the genetic code of a poem, the basic building blocks.

MW: The notion of topicality in poetry seems pretty popular these days. Do you think you have an obligation as an artist to respond to current topical or political situations?

MM: For me, I am not so concerned with topical poems. I don't know. It's hard not to think about this without falling into a kind of cynicism. But there's been injustice of one kind or another since Cain and Abel. While we rightly get upset and want to try and do something about the injustice around us these days, I found that stepping back from the immediate to see the long term is something that I value. For one, it has prevented me from being totally in despair. I think that one of the objects of poetry ought to be the possibility of offering hope or the possibility of offering humor, or a possibility of offering *well, we'll see about that*—something that is capable of transforming the rage so that it becomes something else that is not life-killing. Something that is life-giving. I can't claim to have achieved anything like that, but I will claim to be interested in trying.

If a poem is all reaction and anger on the page and there isn't a simile and there isn't a pattern and there isn't some dynamic between the line and the syntax, no rhythm or anything pleasing to the ear, then the poem is just topical. But the elements of craft can keep a poem relevant even after the topic has passed out of popularity.

There is an intrinsic value in learning how to use the English language. To use the language to express complicated thoughts in lucid terms. We have in our culture at the moment a bunch of people who mangle the language. Maybe they do it on purpose, to obscure what they're really saying. So I think poets have a role beyond trying to make pretty things. We writers, I believe, can set an example as being people that realize that language is a vehicle for thought and expression and a connection to meaning and purpose. And if the people in charge are deliberately misusing language, deliberately manipulating language with the intention of deceit, then as poets, we've got to use language better.

MW: In the last couple of years, you've seen your latest book of poems appear with a new publisher, but you've also had a big life change as well. Has the birth of your daughter changed how you think now as a writer?

MM: It's totally expanded everything. I have a whole lot more to think about and a completely new dimension to feel bound to, as I'm sure every parent has realized. The meaning of your life suddenly changes and you can't go back, and I'm glad. I have absolutely no resistance. It's a wonderful transformative experience. Now that she is two years old, I can't do any work at home when she's awake. That's not a complaint. That's just a fact. I needed to work recently, and I had to go to the public library in Danville to get on top of everything.

MW: You've talked before about how you perceive your first three collections of poems as a type of trilogy "in the voices of three different characters who use their imagination as a way to mediate their immediate circumstances and their connections to the natural world." Then the next three collections of poems you called a mythos of Kentucky, statements on community values and community storytelling. Are you still working in threes? Do you have other trilogies planned?

MM: I think I am probably done with that idea. There will always be some connections between my books, but the idea of playing looser is appealing to me. Those two trilogies were rather exhausting to me. My recent sabbatical project, even though it has some relation to an earlier book of mine, is a totally different thing. I don't want to say too much about it because it's still in process, but I really enjoyed going and getting a hold of something different with that. And then, I'm working with other new poems. I've been working on them through the summer. And then I've got two other manuscripts that are just sitting. They are the poems I've written in the last four or five years. There's enough for two more books, and I'm hoping to make the opportunities to sit down and organize them into new collections. ■

YOKE

JESSIE VAN EERDEN

And there was a woman who had had a discharge of blood for twelve years. She had heard the reports about Jesus and came up behind him in the crowd and touched his garment... And immediately the flow of blood dried up, and she felt in her body that she was healed of her disease. And Jesus, perceiving in himself that power had gone out from him, immediately turned about in the crowd and said, "Who touched my garments?" —*Mark 5.25-30*

Put your hands at the hip yoke, she says, above the lapped V-seam where the skirt gathers then flares. You feel where the womb waits? Where the weight gets carried? This is the center of all gravity. You feel it? She guides his palm with both her hands to the yoke of her dress. The young man blushes and tucks his face away. Her feet are flat on the road, straddling her bicycle, dress bunched up. She releases the warm hand of the stranger walking by and returns her hands to the handlebars.

You feel it, she says, as he hurries off like a lamb.

Every so often along this road by the sea she does this, stops the forward movement of time—time that unmakes our skin and sight and takes in more of our finite heartbeats like someone filling a basket of barley—and she touches a stranger. Sometimes she puts both hands on his face as if a lover, sometimes she traces a woman's life line, sometimes she meets a young man like this one, with a shy face under a derby cap, who blushes when suddenly they are no longer strangers.

She pedals on. The jasmine blossoms quiver in the bicycle basket, peeking from the paper.

■ ■ ■

Can I come? her son asked.

Not this time, maybe next. She kissed his hot eyes, he toddled into her legs to hug goodbye with face and body, all his small strong bones.

■ ■ ■

She pedals on, comes to the wide place at the mountain's base. There is no throng but she pictures the throng. She leans her bicycle against a cedar and departs from its shade into the sun with her cut jasmine. It happened here, and she closes her eyes to hear the voices and scuffling soles, the forceful presence of bodies, and to feel herself again an emaciated husk of woman, eyes hollow, skin like crusts of bread, when she moved through the crowd without memory or plan. And they raised their many voices to someone coming. She saw him in profile, hair simple and dark, shoulders narrow, he was not large. Despite the crowd, he seemed to be among no one, like a man on the shore watching the boats raise their sails. She felt nothing, her fingers curled in like prawn bodies, she was carried by the crowd's current, and he passed by with his simple body walking.

She is in the dust and presses her face to the huddle of tiny blossoms wrapped in paper, white with a blush of yellow at each center.

When he walked by, she felt as though she had passed through a curtain of ribbons each stitched with a line of lilies wilting, like a beaded curtain leading into a backroom but unstrung with beads and sewn with flower petals. Their softness touched everywhere her face, so many petals grazing her face like little hands. The curtain of his sadness—she passed through, and on the other side of the curtain, the air in the backroom was all changed air, charged with her own sadness, her twelve years of hair and flesh going to dull metal, and before that, the years of all she ever was—girl on bike, girl tasting fig, girl spitting venom, girl with hem high slip shown slipped up, woman coming, O the tip of her life—then the menses draining, twelve years *niddah*, untouched, with blood that would not stop.

She is in the dust and presses her face to the huddle of tiny blossoms wrapped in paper...

She stanched it with rags, raw cotton, with sheep's wool. Untouched, she stemmed the flow alone, knitted pads of rabbit fur, scrub grass, moss. She ran from the city when she still had strength to run, out onto the dunes where she let the blood drain out and blacken the sand like animal dung, and she reached down to dip, touched it to her wasting cheeks like rouge, like war paint, like she was mask-making. *Niddah, niddah,* her life iron, her deepest food a filth, drained but never dry. For her inner thighs there was no bath, no *mikveh,* immersion and rising up pure and touchable, only plunge baths in the cattle trough, in the swamp eddies, soaking until she stained the water red and moved on.

Because she felt all that when he passed by with his sadness-curtain of a hundred petals on her face, with his eternity in a viscous skin sack holding all of time so she remembered so he remembered so he could hold her sadness—*because he can hold my sadness*—her hand went out for a clutch of his coat—wait. Wait.

The hem was rough in her hand and it happened in a moment, the backward rush of twelve years, the feel of the inward blooming bath, a wash, up through capillary marrow lobe and dark lip: some girl on bike, some woman tipping falling into green grass, womb like plum and other fruit again, like dawn, like fleshy dawn, or unwithered night.

Who touched me? he asked in the horde that flanked and hounded him on all sides because he knew what touch is. Her lips red with shock. His blush to show the fury of the flood.

■ ■ ■

No one knew her name. When the wind blew west she was Martha, when it blew east she was Beronike and later Veronica, *Vera Icon,* true image, true face. In encyclopedias and church records in basements, in whispers of relics and cloths with secret properties, she was many legends. She was said to be pious, to be there with her white veil to stanch the blood from his forehead when he'd had too much sadness to hold, and the veil she pulled back bore the imprint of his face. In the Greek, in the Latin, in the third-century pages of the bishop Eusebius who went himself to the old Roman city, to the base of Mount Hermon, and said he saw she had made two statues of half-finished faces at the gate of her house: a woman bent, a man about to touch. In brass, in bronze, the bishop wiped the snow from the faces himself, the patina arresting, his own memory suddenly aching.

But no one really knew her name. She had lovers after, she had a child, a son. She put her hand on her boy's head, where he sat with the other children—You feel that? she asked. She fluttered her hand on the top of his coarse cropped hair to say, I choose you—Duck, Duck, Duck, Goose, I anoint you, the center of all, the great risk of joy. And she loved to touch strangers, on the face, the back, the wrist.

■ ■ ■

She leaves her paper of jasmine in the dust and pedals home. She will come again soon with a clutch of lily and rose mallow, snapdragon and phlox, a mayapple with one pop of white—one day maybe with her child. Hyacinths, hibiscus, tulips and the Damask rose, carnations, cabbage flowers sometimes, and sometimes orchid. All the upturned skirts, the cups of want creased at the stem very like skirts at the yoke of the dress—all the blossoms in the basket of her bike for him because he remembers, he whose sadness passes by. Because he knows what flowers are, that they are tiny hands touching. ■

HERE

moonlight on leaves like snow
and chime of owl
from this hollow's heart
under a rib of Humpback Mountain
a late-autumn wind
broke its teeth against these rocks
at sundown
and we lean now, startled by a stillness
that strops our senses keen
until creekfall—a quarter-mile distant—
whispers close as your breath
in this wild embrace

EMILY HANCOCK

WALKING INTO WINTER

Death is opening the paper hearts
of the milkweed, unclasping hands
that held their secret
all summer.
Coated and mittened
against November-cold, I ease
along a hillside path and listen
to the rustle and sift, the small talk
of tall stalks in the wind:

they are shaking out their seeds,
they are lifting their children
into thin air
on filaments of light—
small galaxies
wheeling into the world, each
with one tiny seed-heart
asleep, for now, in the center
of its bright basket.

Tomorrow, the rain
will rinse the empty chambers,
will wash these hollowed bodies
and slowly lean them down
into the fallow field
of winter, that dark cradle
of every beginning.

EMILY HANCOCK

FISH AND WILDLIFE

DEBORAH REED DOWNING

Drew 1957

I was trailing after my father on a path between tall pines, heading back to our cabin at Kentucky Lake. We'd hiked to the bait shop before anybody else had come awake so Daddy could phone Number One. Daddy runs coal mines down in the mountains, and Number One takes care of the coal yard in Lexington when my father takes me and my brothers and Louise fishing. Louise is my mother but she doesn't like to be called that.

From where we were walking, I watched two slick-haired boys in black church clothes striding through the campground knocking on doors. Each boy had a box tucked up under his arm. When they came to a cabin, they stopped, looked one another over and smoothed their hair before knocking on the screen door. A moment later a man in striped pajamas stepped out on the porch. The boys started talking, first one, then the other. I caught my breath, waiting to see what they had in the boxes. The man nodded and hiked up his pajama bottoms; the boys lifted off the cardboard tops. Each boy held up a placard dusted all over with silver and gold glitter. Even in the shade those pictures sparkled like rare fairy dust, the kind that makes wishes come true if you believe. I'm not kidding. I read it in a magazine.

My father was way ahead and I jogged to catch up, watching the powdery dirt puff around my bare feet, gearing up to go lame. When I got close, I slowed and got my mind set. I was about pretending I'd just stepped on the pointed end of a bottle opener, which I actually did once. I could practically see the bottom of my foot squirting blood. I faked a limp, hobbling to slow us down, so the boys would get to our cabin when we did. I wanted to buy one of those posters before my father packed us in the station wagon and lit off for the boat dock. Daddy was striding ahead, whistling, unaware of my condition. He had moccasins on his feet like the ones in a book I got at the park gift store, a true story of how the U. S. Government sent the Cherokee Nation walking westward on a trail of their own cried tears. My book came with a rubber Indian maiden attached to a leather thong that I have vowed to wear around my neck until I die.

Before going lame, I took a healthy leap, trying to put my foot where Daddy's had been. Behind my eyes I watched a brown-skinned Cherokee girl dragging herself through tearful dust, horse soldiers poking her with sharp sticks. I missed Daddy's footprint by a mile, and went back to being crippled.

"I've got something in my foot," I whined. Daddy raised his eyebrows and studied me over his shoulder. I like to look at my father. He is tall and has muscles from hard work. The sun shone through a hole in the trees and settled in his black hair and on his face. He glowed like a picture of Jesus in my brother's Bible story book. My father is beautiful if you want to know the truth.

Daddy shook his head and frowned. "You're dirty as a pig," he said, studying my face as he bent and offered his back. I ran and jumped on, wrapping my arms around his neck, binding his waist with my legs. He loped off bouncing, with a laugh ready to happen. "Which foot?" he said. His voice bobbed happy as a cork when the fish nibbles my bait. "Do you remember?"

"It don't hurt now," I called, bouncing with him, my words wobbling like Jell-O salad.

Daddy slowed to a regular walk. "Better not let your mother catch you saying 'don't.'" Suddenly he stumbled like he'd been shot in a gunfight. "Get down, Drew. I'm too old for this."

I clung even harder. I could feel my father's fast breathing against my ribs. "You're not old," I said in his ear. "You're ripe." He whooped, and began singing about a girl named Molly Malone pushing a wheelbarrow. Sunday nights in summer, when we don't eat anything for dinner but ice cream and I am busy filling a mayonnaise jar with lightning bugs, my father plays this tune on a harmonica. I knew the words but kept still so I could hear his happiness. I wanted everything that was happening right that minute to keep on happening, the two of us headed for the cabin where my brothers would be turning rocks and looking for worms, and Louise packing boiled eggs and celery and leftover fish in the ice chest. I felt so peaceful I forgot about the religious boys; I forgot about everything except loving my father. A few stored up tears leaked out and I licked them away.

Suddenly Daddy changed tunes, spinning around like he was a dancer on *The Lawrence Welk Show*. I lurched sideways, clamped my hands to his neck and held on. "Swing, swing, swing," he bellowed.

"Can we please please see Mammoth Cave on the way home?" I asked. Daddy had promised me the two of us would go on an all-day cave tour on my birthday last year. Mammoth Cave is the biggest mystery I know of, full of Indian bones and artifacts and magic.

The sun shone through a hole in the trees and settled in his black hair and on his face. He glowed like a picture of Jesus...

He staggered to a halt. "I worked in a cave one summer," he gasped.

"You did not!"

He coughed. "Damn it, Drew; you're strangling me!" He pried open my hands and set them on his shoulders. "One summer, before I ever heard of a coal mine, I worked in a cave." He repositioned my feet at his middle. "Signs along the roads announced us," he said, flinging out his arm, pointing at a shagbark hickory like there was a poster nailed to it. He stepped over to the tree and pretended to read. "Swing and Sway with Art Jolly and His Youngbloods." He followed the words with his finger. "Danceland Caverns—It's Cool Inside. I was a Youngblood. I played the saxophone."

"Before I was *born*?" I said. I was always amazed that anything happened before me.

"Before I met your mother," he said. "She swears I made it up. Your mother says there's not a musical bone in my body." I felt his sadness where my stomach pressed into my father's back. I rocked myself to get us back to happy.

My father shook himself like a wet dog does to stop me from rocking, then stepped out, moving his hands off my feet, swinging his arms. We walked past the whitewashed cabins set back under low looping branches. It was quiet in the woods except for my father's breathing and a sapsucker hammering and some old saw-tooth crickets singing in the dry weeds. A breeze stirred the leaves, changing patterns of bright and dark like a picture show. "I practiced on that horn day and night," he said, thinking the memory without me.

"Tell it," I said, urging him with my heels.

"People were desperate in those days," he said. "They needed to dance away hard times, dance their way out of the Depression. Country people who had caves on their farms rented them for dance halls. The wives and kids sold box suppers, fried chicken, pickled eggs and cole slaw and white cake. Darned good economics," he added, with a nod of approval. "Learn that, Drew. Economics is how the world works." He shoved his hands in his pockets and jingled his change. "I played three, four nights a week. Over the mouthpiece on my horn, I watched young men dancing close with young girls in thin dresses and long strands of beads. I craved to get on the floor and dance the night away with a pretty girl."

He slowed and stopped. I felt like he was watching his young self on the path up ahead, and I closed my eyes so I could see him, too. I saw lightning bug lights and red dots floating in the dark gravy inside my head. A mosquito whined at my ear, but I held back slapping him. I needed to hear every word about this mystery father. When I couldn't stand waiting another second, I poked his shoulder with my thumb. "Did you ever get to dance the night away with a pretty girl?"

"Closest I got was one night in the Ozarks when something woke the cave bats," he said. He was walking again, slower now. I saw our cabin up ahead and wondered if the slick-haired boys beat us there. "We were revved up pretty good, playing loud as a big band, when the bats woke up. There were thousands sleeping in the dark caverns behind us and they rushed out at us in squadrons, like fighter planes, swooping and squeaking, diving this way and that, trying to get out of the cave.

"The crowd went crazy. Women screamed and the men jumped up and down, tipping tables, spilling drinks, food. 'Don't stop now, boys!' Mr. Jolly yelled. 'Play on! Play on!' About that time I felt something tickling my scalp. 'Bedbugs!' a man in the crowd yelled. 'These bats are bombing us with their bugs!' He was right! When I got to itching so bad I couldn't play, I called out, 'Sorry, Mr. J,' pulled off my horn, and jumped to the dance floor. I found a pretty blonde whose date had run off and spun her around. After a while the bedbugs quit biting us so bad, and we danced the Charleston 'til sunup."

"Get down, Drew," he said, giving his shoulders a shake. "You're getting too old to carry."

"Ten-and-a-half is all," I said, unwrapping myself and dropping to the ground.

I heard Louise whistling before we got to the screened porch. My mother never sings. She whistles. Complex stuff, like Boris Godunuv, Puccini, Shostakovich, Liszt—melodies I've heard on the radio. I don't think there's anyone in the world who can whistle Russian opera like my mother. Probably nobody's even thought of it. Opera gives my father the stomach ache; he tries not to listen when she whistles. Daddy whistles bird calls when he calls me and my brothers in for dinner. He calls ducks, too, but he has a wooden thing he holds in his lips to make duck sounds. The single most important sound my father makes is a click and suck thing he does when he's troubled and trying to keep it to himself so my mother won't get mad. When my mother gets mad she can't bait a hook without drawing blood. She can't stand up in a boat without wobbling either, but this is because she drinks Manhattan cocktails. Not my father though. At home he mostly clicks and sucks behind the newspaper.

"I love you, Daddy," I called, running ahead. I took the wooden steps two at a time. When I banged open the screen door, my mother stopped whistling. She wet her lips and looked at me in a way I can't explain except to say that things could go either way. I glanced at the table where she was wrapping leftover fish in wax paper. On the table was a paper bag, dark with grease from the fried brim lying on it. Curly-headed Charles William was naked in his high chair. He squealed and stuffed a handful of dry cereal in his mouth, then giggled and spit it back out. Charles William is my baby brother. He is spoiled rotten from being so cute.

Wheeler was bent over the coffee table, working a jigsaw puzzle he won for perfect attendance at Sunday School. He squinted at me through his glasses and stuck out his tongue. Even though Wheeler is a year younger than me and pudgy so he can't run so fast, I am wary of him. Wheeler has a mean streak, and some kind of weird power; when he lies, my mother believes him every time. "Come here," he said, smiling and holding up the top of his puzzle box. "That's what it'll look like when I finish." The box cover showed the picture all worked out; Jesus had golden light coming out all around his head and shoulders, like heat waves, only it wasn't painted on, it was real gold. "Look here," Wheeler said, and opened his hand. He held out a puzzle piece that had the real gold on it. The piece was shaped like Kentucky with the Ohio River running across the top. "I bet it's lucky," he said, putting it in my hand. "Here, you can have it."

Teddy slid out of his chair and under the table like a wet muskrat. "Look," he said, pushing a corrugated cardboard box toward me. Wilted grass lay in the bottom; a yellow-brown terrapin was trying to crawl up the side, his curled toenails scraping the cardboard as he slipped down.

I plopped down on the floor between Teddy and the box. "The turtle wants to go outside, Teddy."

Teddy shook his head and opened his eyes wide the way he does when he's scared. "No, no, no," he wailed.

"Listen," I said. "Remember the turtle with the American flag decal on its shell? The one we got throwing darts at Joyland Park?"

Teddy pinched his nose and made a face. "Stinky."

"He died," I said. "If we take this one home, it'll be a stinky, too."

The problem is that Teddy loves animals to death. He smothered my guppies and neons with fish food and petted five baby chickens to death, one for every year of his life.

Teddy snatched up the terrapin and clutched it to his chest. The turtle pulled in its head and feet with a whooshing, air-sucking noise.

"I got it!" I said, slapping my leg to show what a good idea this was. "We'll paint a 'T' for Teddy on his shell with red nail polish. Then you can put him outside. With that big old T on him, we'll be able to find him easy before we go home." Teddy can't keep his attention on anything that's not in seeing distance. If I got the turtle outdoors, I was pretty sure he'd forget about it long enough for the critter to get away.

Wheeler was pushing puzzle pieces around with his nose, his pinched mouth about an inch from the top of the coffee table. "I'll watch him for you, Teddy," he called out.

"Don't need to," I said. "That ol' nail polish will light him up like a fire truck."

Teddy held the turtle out to me. "Okay," he said.

I turned to Louise. She had finished wrapping the fish and was packing them in the ice chest for our lunch. "Can I use the polish?"

"May I," she corrected. "It's on top of the dresser."

My father untied a loaf of white bread and dropped two slices in the toaster. "I'd like to go to the dock as soon as you and the boys are ready, Louise," he said. "Fish won't bite in the heat."

"Musical theory in action," my mother said, trilling her voice and tossing back her auburn hair. She lifted a newspaper from the table and pretended to read. "Weighted with four little sinkers, the loving couple fish their way through conflict to harmony once again."

"You don't have to go," my father said.

She plucked the last little brim from the brown paper and snapped off its tail with her teeth. "I'm going," she said. "Fishing may be all we have left in common." Sometimes my mother talks in riddles and I figure them out later. For example, a sinker is a little ball of lead I squeeze on the line with my teeth. It makes the bait stay however deep I want it. I think what she meant is that me and my brothers hold her down like that.

Sometimes my mother talks in riddles and I figure them out later.

I heard toast pop out of the toaster and smelled the burn. My father likes his toast black. He says the black is charcoal, and charcoal makes his stomach feel better. He scraped butter on his burned toast with a knife and took a bite, studying the grimace on my mother's face.

Louise patted Charles William's cheek. She picked a bite of brim off the bone with her teeth and fed it to the baby. Teddy inhaled noisily through his mouth. Suddenly Louise pushed back her chair. "I'll be with you in two shakes of a lamb's tail," she said, her voice suddenly sweet as ripe watermelon. Sunlight followed her to the bedroom, passing through her nightgown so she looked like a cardboard cutout. I got the nail polish off the dresser. "Sponge Charles William off for Miss Alice, Drew honey," she said. Miss Alice lives over the top of the bait store; she babysits Charles William when we take out the boat.

"Yes ma'am," I said. "In a minute." I sat on the floor, unscrewed the bottle and took a whiff. The smell reminded me of the hospital when I got my tonsils out. Teddy leaned over the box and watched me dip the brush and paint a thick red line down the turtle's shell. "T for Teddy," I repeated.

Wheeler pushed his foot into my back. "Do it like this," he said, snatching the brush. He dipped it and made my capital T into a little one. He leaned over and blew, his cheeks puffed out like a frog's. "It's a cross like Jesus died on," he said.

Teddy looked back and forth between me and Wheeler, his expression fearful and uncertain. "It don't matter," I said. "It's still a red 'T.'"

"Doesn't matter," my mother corrected from the bedroom. "Drew, are you going to wash Charles William?"

My father put his plate in the sink and ran water over it.

I heard footsteps crossing the porch. A second later somebody rapped on the door. "I'll get it," I said, jumping up.

"Howdy," I said. I gave the slick-haired boys a big smile. "Whatcha got in those boxes?"

"Good morning, miss," the boys said. The tall one took a step forward. "I'm Silas Paltry and this is my brother, Paul Edgar. We're raising money to help the Lucky Stop Methodist Missionary Fund bring the word of Christ to the Dark

Continent! Trade with us and your dimes and quarters will shine for Jesus!"

"Is that dark continent anything like a coal mine?" I asked. "I been in a coal mine. What you all got in those boxes?" Behind me the door squeaked. Teddy grabbed hold of my leg. He was clutching the turtle. "Let go," I said, shaking him off. "I got to look at this stuff."

Daddy strolled out, steam from his coffee cup rising in the air. "Morning, boys," Daddy said.

"Morning, sir," they said, just like a single person.

"They're selling stuff for the dark continent," I explained. "They're about to show their wares." I said wares because my father thinks highly of most anybody selling merchandise and wares is what he sold when he was coming up.

"How's that?" Daddy said with a wink. "The continent of double or nothing?"

"Africa, sir," said the boys. Silas and Paul Edgar looked down at their dusty shoes. I knew nobody had ever said double or nothing to them. I puckered my mouth and held a finger to my lips so maybe my father would stop making jokes.

Then they opened their boxes and each one took out a poster. They were on thick cardboard, twice as big as my school notebook. Mostly they had words on them with a picture at the side instead of the other way round. Silas held up a placard red as a pool of blood.

Paul Edgar's was blue, the exact same color as an Evening In Paris perfume bottle. Words and pictures were thick with glitter—gold on the blood red one and silver on the blue. It took my breath to look at them. Inside, Charles William laughed and threw his cup on the floor. "Can we see all of them, please?" I asked.

My father frowned, and rubbed his chin. "Aren't you supposed to be taking care of something for your mother?"

"Please?"

"This will wait, Drew. Your mother won't."

I ran into the cabin and lifted Charles William out of the high chair and plopped him down in the bathtub where he couldn't get away. I got on my knees and adjusted the water, and scrubbed his face and hands and stomach while he squealed and laughed and grabbed at my Indian maiden. "I can't give it to you, Charles William," I said. "I took a blood oath." When he was clean I wrapped a towel around him, pulled a diaper from the chest of drawers, flopped him on the bed and pinned it on. I set him on the kitchen floor with a spoon and some pie pans and ran back on the porch. The boys had propped the placards along the front of the cabin. They were so beautiful it hurt my throat to look at them. When I let my eyes go out of focus, the pictures breathed with me. At the outside edges of my eyes the trees in front of our cabin were breathing, too. I gave my head a shake. "I want that one," I said, pointing to Evening in Paris.

"Ask the price," my father said. "Money doesn't grow on trees."

"How much is it, please?" I asked. I lifted the blue and silver one, turning it to the sun.

"Fifty cents, sir," the boys said.

"Can I have it, Daddy?" I asked. "I won't ask for anything else, I swear." I knew I would treasure that placard forever, even more than the Indian maiden. When I was a famous jockey with a barn full of race horses, I would hang it at the top of my Christmas tree. That's where it belonged.

My father reached into his pocket. "Keep it in your room," he said. "I doubt your mother will appreciate it quite as much as you do." He winked at the boys again and pulled a silver dollar from his pocket. "Double or nothing?"

Paul Edgar's jaw dropped. He shook his head. "We ain't allowed to gamble, sir," Silas said. "Daddy would flail us."

My father flipped the dollar into the air and snatched it with his hand when it started down. He slapped it on the back of his wrist and held his hand over it. "Heads or tails," he said with a poker face. At first I thought he was joking with the boys, and then I wasn't sure.

Silas and Paul Edgar stood very still. Their faces were shiny with sweat and the grease from their hair. For the first time I noticed how white their skin was. I could see purple blood pump under the skin on Paul Edgar's cheeks. Silas chewed his fingernails like I did, down to the quick. I wondered if they got enough to eat.

My father shrugged, and made as if to go. Silas and Paul Edgar looked to be holding their breath.

"Let me call it!" I yelled.

Daddy glanced at the boys, first one and then the other. They looked so scared of gambling and getting flailed that my stomach twisted up. The sour taste of throw-up rose in my throat and mouth. I can't hardly stand it when my father makes a person feel bad. It about kills me.

"Heads," I said, like a dare, shooting a quick look at him. In his heart, my father is a gambler. He had to see who won. He raised his fingers off the coin, checked it and flipped the dollar to Silas who looked so relieved he almost missed the catch.

The screen squawked and my mother strolled out with Charles William wiggling on her arm. When she bent to set him down her dark hair fell around her face in waves. She had on blue shorts, a white shirt knotted over her two-piece bathing suit. Her stomach was golden brown and flat. She smiled at my father like the rising sun, like right now was perfect and the bad parts of the morning never happened. "What's this, Harry?" she said. "Did you develop an interest in art while I was dressing?"

"Morning, ma'am," the boys said.

My mother raised her hand to keep them from talking. She strolled down the row of pictures, her eyes cast down to see the words. She whistled a snatch of music from "Claire de Lune," a sound so clear and terrible it might have been a bird or a cry for help. "'Our days on the earth are as a shadow,'" she read. I had almost got that one because there was a silver eagle flying across the top, his silver shadow at the bottom. "'Purge me with hyssop, and I shall be clean; wash me, and I shall be whiter than snow,'" she continued. "What's hyssop, fellows?" she said, passing down the line. The boys glanced at each other and began picking up the placards as soon as my mother read them. "'Happy is the man that has his quivers full of them.'" She threw back her head and laughed. "Lord, keep me from those old boys," she said, turning and heading for the steps. "I'm ready to go now, Harry," she said.

She smiled at my father like the rising sun, like right now was perfect and the bad parts of the morning never happened.

"Get Wheeler," my father said, nodding at me, then toward the back of the cabin. I tilted my picture at the sun, squinting to double its sparkle. "Now!" he said.

I tucked the placard under my arm and took off running slow as I could get away with. I wouldn't mind if Wheeler did get left behind.

I found my brother standing under the clothesline in back of the cabin. The line drooped with the weight of wet diapers. There had been a stick propped under the rope and I wondered where it was. Wheeler was holding a thick rock in his hands, staring at something in the grass. "I fixed him like Jesus," he said in a dull voice. "He can't run off now."

The terrapin was nailed to the ground with the sharpened tobacco stick that had held the clothes line, the brown and yellow plates in the middle of his back smashed through by the sharpened hickory. Blood thick as applesauce oozed out around every side of the hole. The turtle's head was twisted out of the shell, its eyes bulging red, the mouth opening and closing with a soft gurgling sound.

I flew at Wheeler straight-armed, pushing his chest as hard as I could. He stumbled backwards and thumped down on his rump, his glasses dangling from one ear, the big rock resting between his splayed legs.

"Why'd you do that?" he shouted. He squinted up at me, like he honestly didn't understand why I was mad. "You damn fool!" I screamed. "You can't go around killing things not like you." I took a breath and stared at Wheeler's blank face, wondering what was inside his head.

I wrapped my hands around the tobacco stick and jerked it out of the ground. The terrapin came with it. A glob of blood dripped off the shell and plopped in the dusty grass. "You tell Teddy what you did and I'll kill you," I said. I shook the turtle in his face. "I'll beat your head in. I'll bash your brains out."

Out front, my father honked again. Wheeler looked toward the sound and got to his feet.

"We're coming," I yelled. My brother plodded off, his hands settling the wire frames of his glasses firm on his ears. I held the turtle in front of me and ran in the opposite direction. I would die on the spot if the poor thing fell off the stick and I had to pick it up. The turtle's head swung limp. I prayed the eyes had shut, that it was dead. I didn't have a plan past running but when I came to the next cottage I stopped. All the cabins are built off the ground, stacked on cement blocks at each corner. I fell on my knees and crawled under the bedroom floorboards holding the staked turtle in front of me.

Clumps of dead leaves were scattered around, rank and moldy, and spider webs everywhere. I raked up a pile of leaves with my hands and buried the turtle under the mound, stick and all. I was shivering and sweating at the same time. Cobwebs got in my mouth and ears. I wanted to sneeze. I closed my eyes to keep bugs out, turned, and started crawling. Before I'd gone two feet my forehead banged a rafter and I fell flat on my face. I groaned, breathing in fungus and dead stuff until the metal pot banging in my brain stopped. I staggered to my feet and ran for the station wagon dusting off my face and arms. My father honked, and revved the engine.

"Damn it, Drew," he said when I climbed onto the back seat.

"Charles William's diapers fell off the line," I lied. "I picked them up." Fortunately, I'm a fast thinker.

"That doesn't make a bit of sense," my mother said. "I snapped clothes pins on every corner." The baby squirmed in her lap, clapping his hands, laughing as he peered over the seat. I leaned closer, wiped my hands on my shorts, and offered him a finger. He grabbed at the Indian maiden.

Wheeler was reading the "Special Loony Tunes and Merry Melodies Fish and Wildlife Comic Book," holding it so I couldn't see his face. On the cover, Elmer Fudd and Donald Duck fished in a leaky boat. Water inside the boat was ankle deep, and Elmer was yelling and bailing with an empty pork and beans can. Donald puffed on a cigar stuck in his bill as he pulled up a fish. He didn't seem to mind that the boat was sinking. I would tell my father what had happened to the turtle when we were alone. I'd tell him I was fearful of Wheeler, how he didn't understand killing animals just because he could was wrong. I'd tell him how I sweated and shivered at the same time when I locked eyes with Wheeler. I was pretty sure I'd tell him. Maybe. ■

THE LEAP

Eighth grader,
older cousin,
clicks her cheek
and kicks
the soft flank lightly;
we jolt forward
faster than breath.
I'm crushed between
her grip on the horn,
hand on the reins,
as the black animal
finds air, whirligig
of mare, sky, ground
passes like integers read
in quick succession.
PVC balances
on the barrels where
my cousin looks back,
as we canter downhill;
how should I know
I cause the thing I fear
the most? Legs rigid—.
The sudden smell
of morning I join
in falling through
the hickory leaves,
the miracle of landing
on our backs unharmed.
The taste of horse
sweat blocks the sight
of the double-wide filled

with aunts: Barbara and Joyce
and Linda and Linda,
their Slims, oblivious I
know the gravity of my body
in the gravity-bound day.

JACOB STRAUTMANN

THE BOY AND THE RAFTER

This was the summer after the winter
the coal stoves of our neighbors upwind
dropped flocks of commas on the parable snow.
Noon crickets slept. The wind abandoned
August and our trailer—that's when voices
lulled me back, pressed my face to a split-glass
window cranked wide to see who I heard,
what had gathered in our new foundation
still cut mud-open. Birds lumbered through
discovering their places amongst themselves,
clumps of rank and retinue, dear purple
draping their feathered congress. How suddenly
silent they were, bowing and sidling like men
unused to looking at each other. What I thought
took on the silver tinge of dream. I doubted
even then what I knew I could never forget,
and I have forgotten everything they said,
their bulbous shifting and speckled necks,
but a cacophony I recall of light opened
to catch the truth, like amethysts
spinning on a necklace of leaving what can
no longer be, and never like they knew it.

JACOB STRAUTMANN

MONONGAHELA, ALLEGHENY COAL FIELD

The season turned them out on their heads.
The kids flicked butts at the tipple and tracks,
with Waylon on the radio, shirtsleeves cut free,
and blew through quick as pick-ups slipping
the valves of some mountain trumpet, rising
chord on chord like pines, like blasted fill,
high lonesome sound of high school football fields,
and higher still, shrinking in the belly of the air

over a city or Great Lake unknown to these
horizons strung three times, tree to tree.
Near the wasp-spangled tool shed, paper
bloat of a late August harvest, someone regretted
each and every year he held onto them like a stone
turning in his belly. He held the answer,
heard the burden once lifted in the wind:
they be gone for good, no chance they stay.

JACOB STRAUTMANN

THIS
MUST BE THE PLACE

JEFFREY HELTON

The clouds overhanging the horizon are the color of coal, and beyond that clot of shadows William can see veins of coursing light--but he spares them no thought. For now there is only the pale sky above and the highway like dark and yellow-lined water passing beneath the old convertible as whips of wind lash joyous against the car, urging it on, sweeping across William's hair and bringing a boy's smile to his tired face until the day's labor of grey seams and shovels vanishes behind him and all that remains is the familiar animal ache of his bones and a longing like a question that only Eleanor can answer. Soon this day will die yet here and now the sun is a golden void, a molten clockface emptied of all markings, and William hollers and laughs, his voice hoarse as he moves parallel these fields where the air is spiced of summer and the birds nest in the amen of sumac and the cows graze and eye him with quiet regard, and everywhere that he looks along the almighty landscape he finds a home, the world itself the greatest among them, a home to the black bears roving the mountain creek beds and the silver trout fated for their maws and the soft-footed foxes that rustle through blooms of pink and red in rhododendron romances. The car is rounding a bend, ascending the hill, and far beyond the curve of a wooden railing the ridgeline is blazed with mountain laurel and azaleas and trees with bloodbright leaves that hint of autumn's coming. William's fingers, nails streaked black, touch the radio dial and turn it until they find a song, its melody timeless, its four chords moving like the calm coupling of lifelong lovers, and though he cannot recall the lyrics he hums that perfect melody and makes up words all his own. An earnest rain is falling when he rolls into the driveway, so he jumps from the car to pull down the ragtop and then jogs for the cover of the porch where Eleanor awaits him, a red kerchief in her hair and dirt at her cheek, and they kiss and she slips the straps of his overalls away and he likewise with her dress and they bring their bodies together like lips to honeysuckle and once they are filled with that cathedral emptiness she says that she has something more to show him. William follows her through the house and then the creaking back door, and below lay four naked garden beds bridged by paths of flat stones, and he sees this space as it is and will be, drenched in color and living light and fragrance, and he marvels at this quiet glory and runs his thumb along the rim of Eleanor's ear with a broad grin on his face, glad to love this woman of strength, cherishing this rain that would nourish all things, even those in the black beneath the ground. William walks down into the yard, and when his feet touch the earth shivers run across his body, and he remembers his grandfather saying that this happens when someone walks over your grave, so William regards the sweep of rain-bowed grass and thinks this must be the place, this must be the place, as if the sky would split above with a bolt for his heart. But it is not yet his time to die, not now, when a lone robin alights on the far fence and Eleanor's legs bead with raindrops and the boards of the garden beds are painted blue like the eyes of the daughter that William will know for too few years and yet love enough for a lifetime, this man who has breathed in the whole of the world, letting the clouds themselves into his lungs, this man less a man than a lightning rod— ■

STYLING MY HAIR, I DREAM OF BEN FRANKLIN

Closest part to the clouds,
you suffer in tedious strands
of moments facing the mirror,
meticulously shaped
to craft that Lego look
of hair boasting suppression.

I flatten you with pomade
and damned if you don't
spring back, as if
some grinning gnome sits
inside and yanks at the filaments
that tie me to weekends, to letting go,
on the windy hilltop flying kites
in a dark azure sky.

Imagine it: unblessed
blowing free, discovering
electricity.

JIMMY LONG

MY SIDE

CHARLOTTE MORGAN

It's taken me four long nights to accept the fact that I don't have to huddle on the left side of the bed anymore. I can spread out. I can sprawl in the middle. I can leave my light on. I can eat chocolate chip cookies on the duvet, or cheesy puffs while I'm under the covers. Nobody will care. Nobody will criticize. Here's the hitch, though: Nobody will even know.

I always slept on my side of the bed, the left. "What's left is mine," I teased more than once in my married life. That's me: slightly snide. Black knew that when he married me, said it was one of the things he loved, my non-Southern-belle bite. Right. Some of my getting-the-leftovers sarcasm comes from marrying a man while he's in his last year of law school. A prescription for problems. One of those hindsight ah-has.

On the other hand, everybody in town thinks they know every little thing about me and Black. And they're all taking sides. Our couple friends Donna and Dickie, who were like, "We will always be friends with both of you, no matter what you decide," are lining up, talking back and forth to one another and one of us daily about who did what when. It's public knowledge that Black has been doing the nasty with his secretary for the last three months now. Willie Nelson called that "the most unoriginal sin," but then Black never did have much imagination. Tax law suits him fine. He has, of course, been forced to reveal his defense to his pals: I cut him off right after the baby and never would let him back in. True. No contest. Try nursing and doing without sleep for six months, not to mention crying for hours on end about the fact that none of your underwear fits. And your new-lawyer husband doesn't come home most nights until nearly midnight. I would've turned to Miss Cleo for comfort before I turned to Black. He's not exactly the consoling type; like, "Come on, Tina. Let's get it on. Please? You'll feel better after." Right. Whine on.

Now that the anti-depressants have finally kicked in, I do miss that part of us, the before-baby-and-sneaky-affair good-in-bed part. But when I'm hunkered down under the covers in the dark missing being touched, I get a clear picture of Black's sweaty bare body humping ol' skinny Marlena and I gag. Almost puke. How could he do that to me and the baby? To us? What a stupid question. How could I have been so stupid?

So when I get up this morning, after I nurse Callie and put her back to bed and take a shower and cry—this going from high as a kite to down in the dungeon is wearing thin, but it's supposed to stop any day now—I decide to get dressed in my hottest outfit and wear my hair swooped down over the right side of my face in that killer wave Black adores. I'll go to his office and confront him. This is ridiculous. We either have to piss or get off the pot, as he has so often told me in his none-too-subtle way.

I intend to sashay past Marlena without even giving her a nasty look; my grandmama taught me, *rise above it.* I will positively float. Besides, it's easy to eyeball some hussy without looking her way. I want to watch that bitch cower out of the corner of my eye, the slutty little homewrecker piece of ass. I've already given her a piece of my mind, and not the piece I cultivated in Sunday School, either. She may be a firecracker between the legs, but there's not too much burning between those freckled ears. Good grief, Black hired her cause he felt sorry for her, what with her runaway druggie ex-husband and those two pasty-pale babies in saggy diapers. I mean, I agreed with him. Like some clueless do-gooder. I was pregnant and hormonal, for heaven's sake. If I was to try a Major Makeover with Marlena, which I wouldn't do in a kazillion years, I wouldn't know where to start: her bitten split fingernails, her tobacco-stained crooked teeth, or that straggly straw hair of hers that hangs all the way down her back like some Tibetan beast.

Marlena Petty—what a name. She's one of those inbred Pettys from around here, in the county outside our home town, where everybody knows everybody's monkey business. It's a wonder she even knows how to turn on a computer; they must teach that to every single body in the consolidated high school these days. Black had to tell her how to answer the phone without using her two all-purpose verbs, don't and ain't. Far as I'm concerned he got what he deserved: trash.

Then again, maybe he's given her her walking papers. When he was carrying on right after I confronted him, he did say he wanted her out of his life. Gone. 'Course he'd like her to disappear. That's a thought that gives me no pleasure. I mean, he screws his secretary then fires her? Isn't that some sort of legal no-no? And him a lawyer? I'll have to crawl back into bed if I keep thinking like this. I do NOT intend to start feeling sorry for Marlena Petty. I want to keep on hating her ugly guts till the end of the world.

I have no idea why I want to go to Black's office this morning. I just do. Trotting after my intuitions has gotten me in a peck of trouble in my life, but I still do it. When I can't seem to resist an urge, I go with it. Why fight the feeling? Maybe I'm getting some sort of delayed energy spurt from the medication. Or the wicked mean part inside me is winning out, or at least gathering steam, and I want Black to face up to what all he's losing. That I am a looker has never been a secret. When I was two years old people would stop my mother in J.C. Penney's,

Trotting after my intuitions has gotten me in a peck of trouble in my life, but I still do it.

ignore my snaggle-toothed brother George, and ooh and aah over me—my thick auburn hair, my milky skin, my too, too sparkly green eyes. I never took any of it seriously; my Mama, quite the beauty herself, said looks never get you anywhere you really want to go. But I know Black's a fool for that very same hair and skin and eyes. Let him eat his heart out.

Or maybe it's 'cause I'm used to seeing him every day of my life—we've been together now for nearly twelve years, half as long as I've been alive. We played together on the block when I was a tomboy and he was somehow the leader of the neighborhood kids the week he moved in. It's like trying to break a bad old habit, like snapping my gum. Once, when he was watching Discovery and I was working a crossword, he yelled out, "That's us, Tina, mated for life." He kept carrying on and pointing at the screen till I had to look up. It was a show about Penguins. Penguins. Imagine that. Life without Black is just plain off-balance.

Or part of it could be needing to tell him that Callie is cutting her first tooth. I haven't answered his phone calls or listened to his messages or opened the door or looked at my e-mails for four days, ever since I found out. He is her father, after all; I will eventually have to talk to him about her. Till death do us part is a fact, not an option, once you have a baby together. And he's got the inside track on the legal stuff. I'd much rather choose the time and place to talk to him than wait for some court to order me. And he adores his baby girl, no question. I know he's called more than fifty times cause of caller ID, and he's come to the door at least ten—I wasn't too prideful to peek out the window, especially in the middle of the night when I couldn't sleep a wink anyway. But I haven't let him in to get his clothes or toiletries or anything like that. Why should I, the lying cheating numbnuts?

I have no idea where he's sleeping, but I'd bet the farm it's not with Marlena. No doubt I have tons of e-mails from him, too, apologizing all over himself. I know he's sorry—sorry as a dog who's caught after he's killed half the chickens, and twice as sorry he let his dick lead him so deep into temptation that he couldn't find his way out before half the town knew. And me. He knows I'm extra sensitive and perceptive and can figure things out way before anybody says a word. That it took me three months is the only surprise. But then I was preoccupied with Callie and my swollen breasts and suppressing the daily urge to kill either myself or Black or the perky nurse in the pediatrician's office. That was before I started taking the Wellbutrin. Besides, luxuriating all over the bed can get lonely, truth be told. All I know is I need to go see him, like somebody with a amputated leg having to scratch it. So I wanna look irresistible. I want him to squirm. And beg. And apologize a million times. But I'd hate for him to cry again. That would be just too awful. Dammit all to hell and back, why is he the one person in the world I need to talk to?

■ ■ ■

I put the car in park and pat my hair: I have not looked this good since I don't know when—maybe our honeymoon to Maui, when I'd starved myself into my size four wedding dress and the five bikinis I'd ordered from Lands End, where you can get the top bigger than the bottom. Not that I don't have a killer butt, cause I do. Just not a wedge, like that J-Lo who thinks hers is so hot. Black's daddy gave us the trip; Black's an only. What else is he gonna do with all his buckets of money? His second wife left him when me and Black were sixteen, and since then he's satisfied himself being a retired bachelor about town. My mama and daddy gave us a knock-down-drag-out wedding reception, me being the only girl, my lame-brained brother George having run off with one of the town sluts so my folks didn't even have to pay for a rehearsal dinner. Those two were way beyond rehearsing anyway, what with their twins already in the oven when they eloped. Good Lord we had fun at our reception. Me and Black learned to dance together when we were kids, and we were way better than Patrick Swayze and what's her name in that movie. We both wanted our wedding day to be one big party and that's what it was, live band, open bar, the works. And our trip could not have been more romantic; I know that's when we made Callie. When I have his attention, he can be the sweetest guy. Could. I must start using the past tense, but it sure don't feel natural. Anyway, the weight has fallen off me while I've been nursing; the only things big, still, are my boobs. Black is a breast man for sure.

I turn the knob, but the door to his office is locked. I try to peer past the Black McDowell, III, Attorney-at-Law sign, make that little tunnel with my hands, but the only thing I can see beyond the frosty glass is the dark. Nobody's in there. At least not in the reception area. True, I am slightly relieved I won't have to see that slut Marlena, but I'm sorta annoyed, too. I was kinda looking forward to lording it over her, me being the legal wife and mother, her being the town scandal. The one I really want to see, though, is Black. My breasts are throbbing right this minute, and I know it's not cause they're too full of milk. I nursed Callie right before I left, didn't even put on my bra or slinky v-neck until I was ready to walk out the door, so I'd be fresh. No leaks. But I have to admit, they hurt, like they need something. Like some gravity pull. I remember clear as glass how they'd feel exactly like this when Black and I were engaged, out dancing at the Satellite, and it'd be late, and everybody would've had one too many beers, and the band would play one of our songs, say Fleetwood Mac, and we'd both be crazy to do it, our hands crawling all over one another. This is different from needing to nurse, more like horny, and I know it for a fact. Why is the damn office closed, anyway?

I'll bang on the door, that's what I'll do. If Black's in there he'll answer. I know him like the nails on my fingers. He'll be hoping it's me and he'll have to answer. He's probably been sleeping on the couch in his office, come to think of it. He'd be mortified, having to sign into a motel around here. The word would be out before he turned the key in the door. I can't see him doing that at all.

He's bound to have heard me. I mean I've knocked at least ten times. I do NOT want to stand out here where anybody driving past can see me. Damn him. Damn him to the lava pits of hell. Where in the devil is he? He'd commit hari-kari before he'd stay at his daddy's condo. And Dickie's wife Donna swore she wouldn't let him stay in their rec room, best buddies or not—over her dead body would she aid and abet a wife-cheater, she'd promised. No way is he with any of our couple friends. And he wouldn't dare be with Marlena, now that everybody knows his dirty business. I would turn into a pillar of salt before I'd drive by her place. He would never be there anyway. Not in a skillion years.

■ ■ ■

I have not gotten gussied up like this for nothing. I wish I had a cigarette; I quit cold the day the stick turned pink. I swear I'd smoke one, right here in my Mustang where I blast anybody who even asks to light up. My blood is pumping now, agitated despite the legal drugs. I could call his cell phone, but I'll be damned if I'll do that. It doesn't have near the impact of showing up, unexpected, in the flesh. What's he thinking, anyway, shutting the office in the middle of the week like there's been some death in the family? Shame on him. Where's his grit? If he's gonna act like some slimy two-timing cheat he ought to at least hold his head up and take what's coming. It's not gonna go away, not in this town. People might could forgive him, him being the golden boy he is, or was, but nobody's likely to forget. He's gonna wear this sign around a long time, so he might as well start getting used to it.

People don't know Black all that well anyway. Not like I do. His handsome, friendly outside isn't all there is to him, not by a long shot. He was way smarter than our valedictorian, stuffy snobby ol' Pamela Parsons. She had her nose in a book all the time; who cared if she was going to Brown on a scholarship? Black did it all—good grades, sports, debate. Course he knew he was gonna be a lawyer, cause of his daddy Senior. The hotshot attorney. Who made everybody call him Senior. He even insists that when Callie can talk he wants her to call him Senior, too, not grandpa. What an asshole. But Black made his own way. He never got over his mama leaving like that, never so much as a postcard after. That so-called glamour puss his daddy married, she could've cared less about Black. Didn't treat him mean, just ignored him. That's almost worse.

He always swore he was nothing like his daddy. Being a part of my wacky family, having his own chosen family, that was more important to him than breathing. I know that. I

I can't just sit here. Everybody in town knows my blue Mustang with the baby seat in back.

know him inside out. Which is why I am mystified about not figuring out this Marlena thing right from the start, right when he had a twitch, before it got so down and dirty. I mean, I knew he was sad and edgy and he'd given up on getting any until I gave the go-ahead, but I figured he was sorta having post-partum depression right along with me. I even suggested he try my legal drugs. I knew from the second she was born and we both got to hold her that Callie is an angel-baby to him, his very own tiny link to what's good in the world. He hates himself for cheating on her, I'm sure he does.

Where in God's name could he be? Black wouldn't run off like his mama, I know that for sure. He'd never do something he despised so much. Course I can't imagine him getting it on with Marlena, either. She must've done some come-on act to get him in the rack that first time.

Stop it, Tina. Stop it right this second. Black is no goody-goody. He's a cheat. And a liar. And you got no right in this world to say Marlena is the cause of it. Act like you've got half a brain, girl. Don't go off half-cocked thinking with your gut instead of your head. Maybe he's the one made it happen, much as that thought makes the bile come up in your throat. Who's to say? She's a homewrecking hag, for sure, but who's to say she lured him on? He's got a mind, besides a dick. She's nobody's pretty thing, that's a fact. Who's to say he wasn't the one came on to her? God knows she was available. And no doubt willing. Still, maybe he made the first move.

I can't just sit here. Everybody in town knows my blue Mustang with the baby seat in back. Good grief, I can hear the talk now: Did you know Tina's stalking Marlena? I have got to get out of here or I'm gonna get the heebie-jeebies for sure. Where could he be? Black would never do anything totally stupid. He's got too much self-confidence. And sense of responsibility. He would never do anything to harm Callie. I know that. But then, I never imagined him having an affair. And where the hell is he?

■ ■ ■

Belinda's kitchen looks like it's gonna cluck any minute, it's so full of chickens and chicken stuff. Still, she is my life-long best friend and I can tell her anything. Plus she won't bullshit me. Ever. Not even now.

"Every single one of the guys thinks Black's a asshole," she says, pouring two tall glasses of sweet tea. "I was talking to Donna last night, and she says Dickie couldn't wait to see him at JayCees, to tell him how screwed up he is."

"So did he?"

"She called back after Dickie got home—we're all clocking the bastards these days, you know. I mean who would have suspected Black?—and said he didn't even show up to the meeting. Dickie's called him a bunch of times, too, at the office, and on his cell, but he won't answer. I don't think he's been to work all week." She gulps the tea; Belinda does everything in gulps. Her frizzy, out-of-control brown hair is bunched on top of her head like a pom-pom. She has worn her hair like this since she was ten—no time to fret with it. Too busy making crafts or painting rooms or, these days, playing blocks with her twin boys.

"So who's talked to him?"

"You mean after he came over here Saturday night and dumped this mess on us?"

"Yeah. I guess. Who's talked to him since then?"

"Nobody. Some of the guys were like, no way, I'm not gonna go listen to the jerk, but Bobby and Dickie have both tried to track him down."

"I went to the office today."

"You're kidding. Why?"

"Don't know. Just need to talk to him."

"Oh, sweetie." I let her grab my hand. I want to be touched by somebody who cares about me. "I have never ever seen two people more in love than you and Black."

I'm dripping tears so I look toward her counter for tissues. She jumps up and grabs some for me, then passes over the whole box.

"Bobby and I have been pretty mad, but we're deep down sad, too. I mean, this messes us all up, you know?"

Now she's tearing up, too, so I pass the box across the table.

I make myself speak; I hate to cry. "Remember at pajama parties how we'd talk about this very thing—how when that manicure gal, that Lorena Bobbitt, cut off her husband's thingy we all laughed and said right on? Give the bastard what he deserves?" Somehow this makes me cry harder, which wasn't at all the way I reacted when I first heard what that half-whacked woman had done.

"What the hell did we know, Tina? We were kids. Besides, if you two can fall apart, it makes anything possible. That's kept me awake every night, thinking."

"You don't think those Petty men would hurt him, do you?"

She cocks her head. "Course not."

"Right. I mean, they're low life and all, but they don't really bother the rest of us, not to my knowledge. They wouldn't come after Black, would they?"

Belinda laughs, nervous-like. "Come after, as in to protect the honor of one of their women? Not likely."

"That's what I was thinking, too. But I can't find him."

"You don't think he's with... her, do you?"

I know why Belinda can't say her name. It sours my mouth to say it, too. "I have told myself a million times, after the things he told me on Saturday, when he was all crying and remorseful, that he wouldn't even want to look at her again, much less, you know, talk to her or anything. But, then, where is he?"

"Oh yeah, when he came over here he was so over her. Like, why did I ever start it in the first place? How the thought of her made him sick to his stomach. How he's dirtied himself and all that by, you know, being with her."

"He wouldn't go to Senior's, not on a bet. Senior probably doesn't even know about us yet."

"Oh he knows, believe me. The legal grapevine is worse than ours."

"True. But Black wouldn't go over there. He has NO respect whatsoever for that daddy of his."

"You want me to call him, see if he knows?"

I look at my watch. My mama's only been at the house an hour or so, but she gets anxious if Callie wakes up and cries, even if she's only wet. "I gotta go in a few minutes."

"What does Mama Sue say?" Belinda loves my mama like her own.

"She doesn't know what to do, either. I mean, she's praying and reading her cards, but she's as broken-hearted as I am, almost. She loves Black. Sometimes I think she loves him more than George, though I know that couldn't be right. It's just George has always been a rascal, and it's been so easy to love Black."

She stares at me like I've discovered truth tonic. "It's been easy for us all to love Black."

I start dripping tears again. "So? Does that mean he gets a pass or something when he screws up big time like this?" I don't mean to, but I'm raising my voice.

She gets up and comes over and pats my shoulder. "That's not what I mean at all, sweetie. None of us are used to Black doing anything wrong. We don't know what to say. What to do."

"Does that give him the right to cheat on me? And make me feel like I can't believe a single word he says ever again?"

"You aren't making sense, Tina."

"How can I make sense out of this? Tell me that." I am full bore crying, now, which always makes me mad as red ants. Belinda knows this; she won't take it personally.

"You have always been the sensible one; you've always had the answers."

"I don't have any now. Not a single one."

"Hey, Black might've been the leader when we were kids, but you came up with all the plans, remember?"

"I guess." Black was always daring, out in front when we played rope swing or rode our bikes out to the country or picked sides for softball, but I was the one to decide what we'd do. We were a natural duo like that, even as children. "That doesn't exactly help right this minute, you know?"

"It doesn't. You're right. But having you sad and helpless and ignoring him, and giving every second of your attention to Callie, Black didn't know what to do, either." She looks at me, hard. "I mean, he was so used to having you to himself all the time."

I glare back. "Yeah, well, the choice he made was disgusting. And I can't believe you'd take up for him."

"Don't get all defensive now. I'm with you, a hundred percent, but I love Black too."

"I don't have anywhere to put any of this. And Lord knows it's the only thing I've thought about for four days now."

"Same with me. Same with all of us."

"This is where I end up every time I think about it. Nowhere. Same place I started. Mad as hell that Black's done this to our lives. Too hurt to think it can ever end."

"So do you still love him?"

I startle. "Course I still love him. It's not a switch I can turn off and on. That's what hurts so damn much. Like, the way I feel right this second, will it ever stop? I hate him and love him all at once. And I've never hated him before, not for one second. I've been mad plenty, but this is way different."

"None of us know how to hate Black."

We sit together sniffling. "I've got to get home. Mama will be a wreck if she's had to walk the floor with Callie too long." We both stand up, and she hurries over and gives me one of her no-holds-barred hugs. "I need to find him, Belinda. I want to talk to him. I don't know what else to do."

"I'll call Bobby, okay? I'll get him to leave the store and go look for Black. Do you want him to come to the house?"

"Okay. I'll let him in this time. Tell Bobby to tell him that. We've got to talk or I'm gonna blow all to pieces."

"Look here, Tina. Feed the baby. Rock her some. Take a nap when you put her back down, okay? You've gotta get some sleep. I'm gonna send Bobby out. He'll figure out where to look."

I shake my head yes and pick up my pocketbook. I think: *Guess I don't look like such hot stuff right this minute.*

"And call me if you need me, promise?"

■ ■ ■

When I open my eyes, the room is dim; he is there, in a chair beside our bed, his head in his hands. I don't mean to feel sorry for him, but in that hazy just-woke-up instant I do. I keep my hands under the covers, though my inclination is to reach out and smooth his hair. Black's hair is always tidy. I can't stand seeing him like this. I stare a few moments before he looks up.

"I knocked; Bobby said you wanted to talk to me. That's why I came on in."

"I left the door unlocked. I was beat." He looks horrible; I know I don't look half this bad. "Have you gotten any sleep?"

"I went in to look at Callie. I was quiet, I swear. I had to see her. God, she's perfect. We did that right, didn't we?"

"Black, we need to talk about all this. We need to deal with it. Saturday I was crazy mad, crazy hurt. I couldn't—"

"I'll never forgive myself for what I did to you, what I did to us. I swear, I don't know how I did it. I can't stand myself."

I push myself up on my hands. "I know that. I know you, Black."

"I don't even know myself any more. I don't want to know myself."

"We've got to take a look at all this and deal with it, Black. It's not gonna do anybody any good for us both to keep wallowing around in it."

"I thought I was sad before, I thought I was unhappy. It like to killed me, you looking right through me after we brought Callie home, like I wasn't even here. But I don't think I can stand how I feel now. I hate myself, I hate feeling this guilty and worthless—"

"Shut up!" I pound the bed with my fists. "Shut up, dammit, and listen to me!"

His face is stunned, like I've smacked him, but he stops talking, thank God. I can't stand to listen to him feeling sorry for himself. "You are so pathetic. First you aren't man enough to wait while I get over having the baby; then you spend all this time feeling sorry for yourself after you screw around with some slut for three months. You make me sick!"

He keeps staring like a child caught playing doctor.

"Don't you dare say a word. I swear, I might start throwing things if you say a single word." He shakes his head, I guess to let me know he won't speak. I don't need his damn permission anyway. "I have been sick to death, sicker than I was when I was so depressed, sicker than I've ever been in my life. And it's all your stupid fault. Do you hear me?"

I don't mean to feel sorry for him, but in that hazy just-woke-up instant I do.

He nods yes, finally closes his mouth.

"And I have no idea when I will forgive you. It might take forever. I don't know."

Now he looks puzzled.

"I will try, damnit. I will try to forgive you for acting like some horny sixteen-year-old. I have to. I don't have any damn choice."

Now he shakes his head, whispers, "But why?"

"I love you, dammit, Black. And you love me. I know that. I know it in my insides, in every damn cell in my body. And you know it, too. But I will not stay married to some whipped puppy pathetic baby who won't act like a man and get himself together. I am furious with you; I am so mad I could spit at you right this minute. You ran away, do you realize that? I had no idea where you were? I like to lost my mind, today, when I couldn't find you."

"I thought you couldn't stand the sight of me?"

"I couldn't, dammit, just like I didn't want to have sex with you for six months. But you are my husband, goddammit, despite what you did with that Petty bitch. You need to be my husband and stop running away when it gets tough around here. Stop running away when I need you the most." Now I am crying, and I can't stand that. "Where the hell were you, anyway?"

"I was at George's. He was the only one I knew who wouldn't throw me out."

I hurl a pillow at him. He lets it hit his shoulder and fall to the floor. "I should've figured that out, damnit. That makes me so mad. That weasel George should've told me."

Neither of us says a word.

"I don't know what I'm gonna do right this minute, Black. My head is a mess and I have cramps and all I want to do is sleep. But I am not going to give up, I know that. And if you give up you are not the man I've known half my life, not the person that knows me better than I know myself."

"I am so sorry—"

"That is the last time you will say that, do you hear? Right now you are a sorry sleaze of a husband and we both know that." I am so worn out I can hardly finish, but I have to. "But I want our life back. I want you to be Callie's father, for her to have you here, not off in some apartment with a new girlfriend every other month. I will not let this ruin me, ruin us."

For the first time I see something in his eyes I recognize, something that's not wounded and empty. Some glimmer of the Black I know.

"You can stay here 'til she wakes up. You can bring her to me. I need to get some sleep. Then go back to George's. Get yourself together. Get back to work."

"I will."

"That woman, you'll have to find her a job. Give her a whatchamacallit, severance pay. It's not right, what you've done. Not one single thing about it is even close to right."

"I know."

"But she can't be part of our life. Not for another second. I won't allow it."

"I don't know how to wipe it out of my mind."

"You'll just have to find a way. Talk to somebody. But we've got to put it behind us or it'll never work."

"Can you do that, Tina?"

It's the first time he's said my name, and I realize what a relief that is, what a tiny breath of a beginning.

"I said I would try, dammit. Now stop acting helpless. You've never been a crybaby and I won't put up with it. Plus you have to go talk to my mama. She is beside herself."

He puts his head back in his hands, shakes it back and forth. "I know. I will."

"Quit that. Just quit it. If you're going to turn into some sniveling moron you can leave right now. I said I wanted you back. I mean you, Black McDowell, not some pathetic pity person."

He stands, reaches his arm toward me, but I flinch. "Don't. Don't you dare touch me. I'm nowhere near ready for that. I have no idea how long this will take, like I said, and I can't believe I'm even talking to you, to tell you the truth, but I had to face it today, to tell myself the truth: I've missed your sorry ass."

His eyes look straight into mine, grateful, amazed. "You did? You swear? I don't deserve—"

Damn straight, I think, but I don't say it. "In some ass backwards way we deserve each other, Black. And love each other. We've sure as hell screwed up, though, both of us, and I don't understand it one bit. Right this minute I am so furious, still, I could scream half the day and not be done with it, but I'm too damn tired." I am so exhausted I can't say another word. I slide under the covers, pull them up to my chin, and know I will finally rest. I close my eyes. I sense him; he is still standing there, still looking at me.

"I love you so much," I hear him whisper as he tiptoes across the hall to Callie's room.

I turn over and pull his pillow up under my head, then burrow down in the middle of our bed, one deep breath away from sleep. ■

HAY ROLL CALVING

Hay roll tractor
totters around the slope
like an old farmer in a hat
leaning on the setting sun
turning slowly to follow
long brown trails of raked hay.

He scarfs it up,
Leaves the field clean,
digesting until slowed to
a thoughtful pause
lifts the tail hood,
and calves the roll
onto the ground
with great relief.

Then indifferent, turns away
onto another row
circling the field
to get progeny more.

Comes morning,
a scattered herd
of perfect, round bales
are populating the hill,
sculptures of a mind
that sees the world is round.
And the rising sun too
with a round face smiles.

BR. PAUL QUENON

STUDY IN EMPTY BOTTLES

After work,
through the evening
until the TV was but a flicker
in the night window,
Daddy would line them up
across the table.

Each drained beer bottle.
received a belch and sigh,
welcoming flair
before he whittled
a treasured place
in his new design.

Enablers,
we would bring him
the next cold one
like clay or paint
for an eager master,
careful not to jar
his skillful creation.

Every so often,
before he passed out,
he would cock his head
in wonder at such art,
at what muse might
applaud the drink.

Mama dismantled
his geometric handiwork
each hectic morning,
bottles we kids
would have to haul
out to the garage.

It never seemed right though,
like splotching a Rembrandt,
taking blade to Picasso,
blighting what a man
took pride in crafting,
his presence so carefully
carved into the world.

ALLISON THORPE

AND THEN THERE WERE TOMATOES

Summer brags outside the tall windows
Inside, the air chatters winter

Our workshop assignment:
Describe something lost

Into this season of sun and longest days
I write about tomatoes

Planting them in my journal of absences
Alongside whippoorwill and gypsy breeze

No room for their sprawl of limb and fruit
In this corseted world of concrete angles

The pen in my hand now a stick I poke
In the dirt of garden memories

How in our first year of not knowing
We filled row after hard worked row

With their leafy zest among wire enclosures
Dreaming the wealth of sauce and salad

Of sealing that lavish flame to jars
A primal passion to melt any snowy horizon

How soon those wire cages groaned
With the swell of animal wildness

The redness a blundered sea
With no hope of parting

Our lives became a slaking
An orbital glut of flesh and skin and seed

Even the chickens turned away
From our lavish offerings

Every measured garden after
Brought laughter for such innocence

But then we remembered that first ripeness
That plump of sun you placed

Childlike and warm into my hands
The mouth of summer singing

ALLISON THORPE

A COUNTRY OF EDGES

SEAN PATRICK HILL

I had not lived there a week before my feet wore a path from my door to the pond-side; and though it is five or six years since I trod it, it is still quite distinct. It is true, I fear that others may have fallen into it, and so helped to keep it open. The surface of the earth is soft and impressible by the feet of men; and so with the paths which the mind travels. How worn and dusty, then, must be the highways of the world, how deep the ruts of tradition and conformity!

—*Henry David Thoreau,* Walden

I

The villagers of nineteenth century Massachusetts were generally not a people who loved the woods. Aside from a woodlot, a stream to power a mill, or ground that might be cleared to farm, there was little profit to be found in the forests and mountains. By and large, the pragmatic New Englanders were not a kind of people to wander aimlessly among the trees, sketching flowers. For this reason, Henry David Thoreau was an oddity.

The people of Concord, as Thoreau noted, clung largely to the town and its commerce. By the time Thoreau arrived on the pond in 1845, a change in attitudes toward nature, especially among writers and artists, was only then beginning to take deeper root. Thomas Cole had just begun his painting of the Catskills, founding what would be known as the Hudson River School, and Emerson's *Nature* had been published less than a decade before. Americans simply didn't think of the woods yet as a retreat, let alone a place for recreation. Thoreau was among those describing what the ordinary citizen of America was slow to realize: the value of nature beyond our commodification of it. Given the attitudes of the time, Thoreau's revolutionary proposition for Americans, at least in part, was that there was more to nature than land to farm, trees to harvest, or granite to quarry. No wonder people thought him idle.

In the fall of 1867, John Muir would have appeared equally strange when he began his extended hike from Indiana to the Gulf of Mexico, documented in his book *A Thousand-Mile Walk to the Gulf.* His long sojourn was an utterly transcendental experience, if not a lonely one, transcribed into his journal in lush and detailed phrases alongside his pressed flowers. To see such a traveler—he didn't even have a horse—in the South in the wake of the Civil War must have seemed incredible. After all, the woods teemed with armed outliers and thieves. To be so bold as to travel alone in what was still largely a wilderness must have bordered, to the common mind, on stupidity.

Muir and Thoreau's compulsion to record, to save for posterity and, ultimately, to share through publication the wonders of the natural world, is a sentiment I well understand. I appreciate their records as a reader. A colleague once loaned me Muir's *Thousand-Mile Walk*, published posthumously, to read as an introduction to Kentucky, to which I had only recently moved. Muir knew the names of the flowers, and I didn't, and therefore my reading this book, a kind of early guide to the region, was edifying.

But as a writer myself, I also find purpose in sharing my findings. Writing about trails, I could almost think of myself as a scientist, a researcher publishing papers. In 2011, my enthusiasm for Kentucky's Red River Gorge and the undeniable urge to describe it, to inform readers of a place they should see and experience for themselves, verged on obsessive.

Had John Muir, on his journey southward from Indiana, jogged a few hundred miles to the east, he might have seen what is now the federally designated Red River Gorge National Geologic Area of Kentucky. This roughly forty-four-square-mile circle of sandstone arches, imposing limestone cliffs, and dense hardwood forests would have been a wonder to him, along with the endangered white-haired goldenrod. Likewise, at the time of his journey, he would have seen precious few people in the Gorge, either along the river or in its "hollers." Though remains of the Adena Indians have been found buried in its abundant rock shelters, the modern Shawnee and Cherokee tribes seem to have rarely, if ever, passed through the Gorge. The *Athiamiowee*, the "Warrior's Path" traversed by both tribes, crosses the Red River downstream but did not go through the Gorge itself.

As for white emigrants, there would have been few, as the influx of settlers to this largely inaccessible land was, for the most part, yet to come. Most, at any rate, were bound for the Bluegrass to the west, where forage and game were abundant. Had Muir followed some of the creek branches to their headwaters, he may have found slim evidence of human use such as the remnants of Civil War niter mines, the rock scoured for the manufacture of gunpowder. Despite the numbers of settlers who did homestead throughout the Cumberland Plateau, he would have had the Gorge largely to himself.

By the time Muir's book was published by the Sierra Club in 1916, farming would have been far more common on the flats along the Red River, and logging in the Gorge was to prove itself the dominant industry. When the Bluegrass Group of the Sierra Club's Cumberland Chapter was founded in 1968, the Gorge had long-since been razed of its timber.

In the 1960s, the Red River found itself under what was perhaps the biggest threat it had faced when the Army

Muir and Thoreau's compulsion to record, to save for posterity and, ultimately, to share through publication the wonders of the natural world, is a sentiment I well understand.

Corps of Engineers concocted plans to build a flood-control dam in the Gorge. This structure that would have effectively submerged a significant portion of the area, including many of its low-lying arches—the highest concentration of sandstone arches east of the Mississippi—as well as its creeks, bottomland forests, phoebe nesting sites, and archeological finds yet to come.

The narrative of this narrow-minded endeavor was not unlike the famous story of John Swift who, based on a dubious tale he once heard, came to the Red River in the 1760's in search of a reported silver mine somewhere in the Gorge, an expedition that was continually thwarted and ultimately a failure. The Army Corps of Engineers undertook their quixotic campaign with similar fervor but unlike Swift, they were thwarted not by the clifty geography or errant maps. Instead they were challenged by locals who would have lost their farms, and hence their livelihood, to the flooding, as well as Kentucky's burgeoning environmentalist community.

In the ensuing decades, after the plan had been shelved, several books were published about the Gorge, including Wendell Berry's seminal *The Unforeseen Wilderness* and, by the turn of the century, the Bluegrass Chapter's *Hiking the Red: A Complete Trail Guide to Kentucky's Red River Gorge.* Recreation had become the new industry of the Gorge, numbering among its customers fishermen, campers, auto tourists, rock climbers, backpackers, and day hikers. By the summer of 2011, with a signed contract for a popular hiking book press, I was poised to make my contribution to the further advertising of the area which had seen its archeological sites littered and plundered by visitors and locals, its topsoil and timber denuded by ignorant land use methods, and its delicate sandstone outcrops pocked with carved names and profanities for decades. The Red River Gorge, as the Bluegrass Chapter had warned in their trail guide, was already being "loved to death." I wonder how I've contributed to this.

■ ■ ■

II

The paradoxes with writing a guidebook to a place are many. Consider the number of reasons we go to a forest—to the Red River Gorge, for example. We want, certainly, to be exposed to beauty and grandeur, but there is also an undeniable urge to simply be alone. That is exactly what Thoreau wanted at Walden Pond. Muir, too, is famous for his solitary wanderings of the Sierras. Now consider the core American myth of the wilderness, one as much in place today as it was in Thoreau's mind of the time: the wilderness as a place of retreat from society, as a way to commune quietly with oneself—as a way, in short, to escape. Given the increase in visitors to the Red River Gorge, one wonders if this escape is even possible at all.

Though Muir may have found it in Yosemite early on, today the experience of solitude there is fleeting if not outright impossible—little wonder that Edward Abbey's prescription for the iconic national park was to simply remove the roads. The great granite valley of the Merced River is not as it was for John Muir (or Teddy Roosevelt, for that matter), just as the Red River Gorge is not what it was for the prehistoric Adena Indians, or the early land surveyors, or the farmers, timber fellers, and moonshiners—not even for John Swift and his elusive silver mine.

At the same time, the wilderness is also associated with fear, a vestige of Puritan paranoiac thinking, in which the woods are full of danger, even outright evil, in the forms of wild animals—the wolves, mountain lions, and bears that have been common in Kentucky— and the vague *Other*, especially as personified by other people. Once settlers feared the Shawnee and the Cherokee in the Kentucky country—"The Great Wilderness" as the long hunters were wont to call it. But now hikers fear running into gun-carrying locals or, as I've experienced, meth-addled addicts. There is also the fear of the unknown itself. No one wishes to be lost in the woods. Rather than relying on a map and compass, virtual antiques in the age of smart phones, we now turn to the handy trail guide and GPS units to alleviate our anxiety.

Either way, we want desperately to maintain solitude. Every hiker knows the feeling of coming across a family of hikers, kids in tow, shambling along. Such interactions are often a different affair if these other people are traveling in the opposite direction, but they tend to be most unwelcome when we realize they are going our way, have unleashed dogs, or are talking loudly on cell phones. We might find ourselves offended, as if that trail belonged to us somehow, as if it were our right to be there alone. This may be the reason I've noticed people wearing earbuds in the woods: in order to find their Walden experience, to roam the pine-laden ridges as if no one had been there before, they simply blot out all potential interaction.

What happens, then, when one writes a guidebook? Or more precisely, when I write a guidebook for the Red River Gorge, one of the most heavily used recreational areas in the state of Kentucky? For one thing, the author charts a route for others to follow into the wilderness, or else the "wilderness experience." One gets a chance to play Daniel Boone—in my case, in Boone's own backyard. When I told others of my plan to write a hiking guide for the Gorge, they found it odd; for the Red River Gorge, there were no less than four guidebooks before I came along with my contract, though some were, admittedly, outdated or out of print. At the same time, I insisted that much of the Gorge was still undiscovered—at least by outsiders. Many trails were understandably untrammelled, as opposed to those paths to the most famous sites like Gray's Arch or the Auxier Ridge. There were many times I hardly saw another soul hiking. In time, that would change.

In the 1960s, before the real start of the widespread "Outdoor Recreation" culture we now know and are marketed persistently, the Red River Gorge was known mostly to its inhabitants. It was the Army Corps of Engineers with their plan to build the dam in the Gorge under the guise of flood control that drew attention to it. When the scheme was soundly defeated, or at least indefinitely shelved, people began to go to the Gorge for weekend trips. Even then, the littering had begun in earnest.

Trashing our wild places seems impossible to avoid as long as people maintain an image of those havens as a respite from society, as an escape from our problems, even if for an afternoon, but consequently bring along their already negligent ideas that make throwing garbage on the ground a casual thing. Still, nature can be a respite if approached respectfully; the problem is, in part, the great industry profiting from this drive to escape. Indeed, the Army Corps of Engineers had this in mind in their plan to flood the Gorge, drowning its arches, its animal habitat, its archeology and complex human narratives for a purpose—they looked forward to a recreational lake, and business interests were already lining up to sell boats, cabins, and experiences.

But now the Gorge has become something else, or rather many things. It is a place to camp and to build a fire, of course. It is also a place to drink beer. It is a series of cliffs to rock climb and, increasingly, from which to tragically fall. It is a river to canoe, or to fish, and it is a network of trails to hike or bird watch or flower hunt, all of which come with their inevitable checklists often taken from guidebooks. There's nothing wrong with that, in and of itself, but we so easily default into thinking of places in terms of things to check off: how many trees we know, arches we've seen, trails we've hiked. Or where the berries are, where the best pitches are—or fishing holes or postcard vistas, all of which, in our minds, suggest that we have truly been to a place, have experienced it, and have even *entered* it. All of this is suspect.

This leads to a sense of *ownership*. We want the Red River Gorge to ourselves, feeling we deserve it, and we would be happy to run off the beer drinkers, the groups of twenty backpackers slowing our gait, the rock climbers who clog parking lots and take up camping sites on October weekends, or those that would keep us from digging for artifacts, carving our names, or killing dens of rattlesnakes because they offend us. No wonder most guidebooks make the simple suggestion of hiking during the week rather than weekends, as my own does—they sell an experience of solitude, of ownership.

I would like to think my book is different. It walks a fine line between telling readers which trails are likely to offer solitude and encouraging exploration to appreciate the place's splendor. Although I, too, want an experience of solitude, at the same time I enjoy writing about trails, which is to say I want to share information about them—perhaps a vestige of the high school teacher in me. My writing is, if anything, enthusiastic. I feel the need to share these places, to tell people of their wonders, to say, *go and see for yourself.* Inevitably, I have no control over those who hike with respect and those who leave energy bar wrappers along the trail—or plastic water bottles, or even what Wendell Berry described memorably as the "lavish blossoms of pink toilet paper." I may climb to Signature Rock with the ideal of a wonderfully lonely experience at the rim of a cliff and find, instead, a family of hikers with my book in hand, spitting sunflower seed shells over the edge.

■ ■ ■

III

When I first set my eye on the Red River Gorge, I had the optimistic feeling that the enormous task of documenting the entire official trail system of the Geologic Area, as well as the bordering Clifty Wilderness and Natural Bridge State Resort Park, would lead me to some sort of personal transformation, a radical change stimulated by a discovery of nature on a new level. After all, writing a book requires due attention. However, what Wendell Berry called "A Country of Edges" became for me a country of lines linking Point A to Point B. If there was any "edge" to it, it was simply the drop-off—whether precipitous or not—that fell from either side of the trail. I stepped to the side of the trail from time to time, but usually with a purpose in mind: to take a picture, to check the GPS device, to have lunch, or simply to rest. But the great mass that was the deeper wilderness of the Red River Gorge, all of it off-trail, was beyond me. In order to write my guidebook, I had to stick faithfully to the "ruts of tradition" laid out by the U.S. Forest Service, the sixty miles or so of trail that threads the ridges and hollows of the Geologic Area, in addition to those in the nearby state park and wilderness area. Thus, I wrote a guide to *trails*, not a guide to the wilderness.

A typical hike in the Red River Gorge, for me, went like this: I'd show up at the trail at dawn, perhaps having driven 150 miles mostly in the dark. I'd park at the trailhead and, as my editors suggested, I paused to give my Garmin GPS device time to locate its satellites. While it did I geared up, making sure I had my notebook, at least two or three working pens, my point-and-shoot camera, and extra batteries for the GPS.

When my laces were tight, my hiking poles extended and secured, and my pack loaded with lunch and water, I would stand at the exact beginning of the trail. Before I even began walking, I would write down the coordinates in my notebook and begin what is known as a "track," a detailed route on my GPS device. Once I had the track started, I made the first of many "waypoints," designated by little blue flags on my now-evolving map and which pinpointed not only trailheads but also junctions with other trails, stream crossings, viewpoints, and other points of interest. Each time I did this, I would need to stop, which in terms of the Red River Gorge could mean a ponderous interval of key-punching and note taking while furiously warding off mosquitoes or deer flies. At the end of the hike, I would stop the track and place one final waypoint. At best, this should be a quick, effortless task.

However, the Red River Gorge has numerous problems with GPS mapping. For one, tree cover is notorious for bad readings. Secondly, much of the Red River Gorge consists of coves or hollers, where surrounding ridges can impede the satellite signal. The Whittleton Branch Trail took me four tries to get right: first because the GPS's batteries ran out, second because I lost the signal without knowing it, and third because I ran out of storage space on the device. I got to know that trail well and I learned to watch my step— once I almost walked on a drowsing copperhead.

I saw arch after arch, waterfalls and flowers, and I paused beside many creek-cooled grottoes, but I rarely got to enjoy them.

The true cost of mapping a trail is one of attention; that is, my attention was devoted to mapping and documenting the trail rather than paying attention to where I was. Sure, I'd look around, peer over vistas, and stop to look at a millipede on tree bark. It's just that I couldn't stop to study the bug, let alone identify the tree. No matter what happened, because I had such a distance to travel to get to the Gorge and back home again, and because time was limited—I worked several jobs in addition to graduate work and being a father—I often simply had to plow on through the hike, to get the information and get out. I figured throughout my sojourns, if that is in fact what they were, that I was giving the place a once-over, that I could always come back. Better said than done, as it turned out.

I saw arch after arch, waterfalls and flowers, and I paused beside many creek-cooled grottoes, but I rarely got to enjoy them. It took me a while to realize that I was not at all exploring the Gorge, but making a commodity of it, reducing it to a task to be done for an advance-against-royalties check, a publication credit, a future career in writing—a series of distractions, really. And the ultimate distraction was what stood before me every time I went: not just the place in its fullness, or the intimate details of a spicebush swallowtail on a roadside weed, but the time I had to spend or waste. I got so wrapped up in the fact I was writing a book that I missed the Gorge itself. I moved through it at the speed I raced down the Mountain Parkway, both coming to the trail and heading home, a four-hour round-trip. I learned there is little difference between *writing* a guidebook and *reading* one: you're still moving linearly.

The poet Gary Snyder once pointed out the difference between Native Americans and the heirs to European colonial thinking as a difference in, among other things, perception of space. We moderns—as well as our forebears who explored the wilderness in search of gold or land or simply a new life—tend to move, Snyder notes, from place to place on a line. This implies an objective, a goal, a destination at the expense of truly understanding what it is we are moving through, an end-point that for many of us implies a point of arrival, an achievement, if not our own little Eden. Native Americans, on the other hand, move through space as the locus of an ever-expanding circle, which encompasses a full range of knowledge—a method of understanding in which the traveler is fully involved in the landscape. Being at the center of such a circle in the Gorge would mean knowing that Laurel Ridge is good for blueberries in summer, or that Martins Fork will be high in spring, that rattlesnakes den in the sand by Swift Camp Creek; that the stands of trees will tell us our elevation, what kind of soil we are walking on, and what its nineteenth-century history of logging may have been.

But as Wendell Berry points out in his book on the Gorge, we inevitably *drive* to places like the Red River, at sixty-five miles an hour or so, and when we park our cars and start off on the trail, our minds are still going at that speed. We've not had enough time to leave behind the very things we wish to escape, and so we are still troubled by songs we heard on the radio or a lesson plan that needs tweaking or a chiropractor appointment that needs to be rescheduled. We never slow down and enjoy where we are, let alone *enter* it.

No wonder I was so sorry when the hike was over. When I got home I wanted to return to the Gorge as soon as possible because I was never really there in the first place. Instead, I moved through my experience of the wilderness on a line, in a rut of tradition (here is where we have decided to walk) and, worse, conformity (this is the trail we all walk, never mind the unmarked trails or the vast, frightening blank spaces in the map), taking pictures along the way of things I saw in passing. I've often imagined that the dictum of "take only photographs" meant I could take such sacred places with me, preserving the experience through pictures. But the experience is to be had in the moment.

The great enemy to our experience of the wild is simply *time*. It takes time to be in a place, time to stop and consider the sound of a falling stream, how its timbre changes inch by inch. It takes time to stop and notice how different the sound of wind in October poplars is from wind through winter pines. What guidebook can describe this? How many pages must such a field guide contain?

The end of linear thinking in the wilderness becomes a notion not unlike that of "peak bagging," such as a Coloradoan checking off each 14,000-foot summit they climb— itself a sort of conquest, an ambiguous kind of silver lode. Such conquests can quickly become obsessions, become the only destination, the ultimate Point B. John Swift likely saw little of the country save his own dream of riches. But hiking is no less susceptible to this line of thinking. In the process of writing a trail guide, I naturally fell prey to linear thinking, to a kind of "trail bagging" ethic in which I knocked off track after track then congratulated myself on my increased "understanding" of the Gorge. I couldn't see all that I had missed, focused as I was on my GPS device mapping my line for the day, making of that line a monument. In the end, I would write a guidebook to a linear perspective of the wilderness, one that would lead other people into the same quicksand in which I myself had foundered.

A guidebook serves many purposes, and though its primary *raison d'être* seems to me a pre-packaged experience, the deeper reason serves to remove the fear from the unknown. Despite the occasional run-in with a viper or a black bear, a trail is basically *safe*. We still inhabit a fear of the wilderness, a distrust of dark corners, and a trail guide is really an instruction manual for touring, for seeing the sights without the attendant anxiety, frustration, or difficulty of discovering the nature of a place for oneself. And here is the bottomlands of our psyche: as consumers, we simply are conditioned to be told what to do, what show to watch, which cola to buy, which arch to see and on which trail to see it.

The language of the guidebook follows suit; what we are really looking for is a *description* to assign to our experience, even a phrase, a word: Sky Bridge, for example, or Chimney Top Rock, mountain laurel, screech owl, shale. As if simply by invoking the words "Gray's Arch," we could suggest that we have been there, experienced it, understand it. But as with all language, we are using someone else's words, inherited words to fit an inherited experience. How different it is to say, "I've hiked the Courthouse Rock Trail" rather than "Standing in the rain, in a grove of flowering rhododendrons, I saw a red-eared slider in a creek." It's the difference between reportage and poetry.

It occurs to me now that the hiker—or by extension, the consumer of nature—is caught in a hall of mirrors; for one thing, in order to map the trails, I myself had to consult other guidebooks, other maps, other people's designations of value. A heavy responsibility weighed on me, in that I was now the purveyor of experience. The hiking guide resembles a self-help book, an efficient way to make a change in one's life and understanding with a helpful author who has supposedly traveled the country of the mind and has insights to share. But the map is never the territory, in either the wilderness of the mind or the wilderness before us. To deviate from a given, plotted, and GPS point-checked map is to enter our fears naked. But it is also the doorway to a true experience and, ultimately, to freedom.

Many years ago I backpacked in the Diamond Peak Wilderness of Oregon with my brother, Michael. We camped on a lake that happened to be the terminus of a Forest Service trail and so, it seemed, there was nowhere else to go, no further we could push—a limitation of trail-based thinking, of course. But he was competent with both map and compass, and we decided to go cross-country—really, uphill through the forest—to find a number of small, unnamed lakes. He taught me the basics: how to orient the map and set the compass, plotting our course simply by sighting one tree to the next. Before long, we were far from the lake, far from any trail, in a world of fallen trees, mounds of bear droppings, and unmapped gorges. We had gone a ways and not found the lakes, and if there was any disappointment, it could only be that of persistent Point B thinking. So he told me to wait while he scouted ahead. For a time, I sat on a log in the silence, and the feeling that rushed in upon me, however momentarily, however fragmentary, was that of isolation in a pure wilderness. I felt uneasy.

We never found the lakes, but that didn't matter. All I remember is that feeling of being alone in a forest at last—one of the most enduring reasons people come to the wild, and the most difficult destination of all to obtain, let alone to hold onto.

Another time, hiking in the Gorge up the Whittleton Branch in the dead of summer, I met two men coming down. They told me that the wooden beams across a portion of the trail, where a number of seeps muddied the path nearly year-round, were actually remnants of the old logging railroad that had passed through this ravine. I hadn't realized this. Then they told me where to find a massive rock shelter, in which someone had built a throne of limestone. They described it simply: listen for the waterfall; when you hear it, watch for a small user trail over the bank, and go down through the rhododendron tangle, then cross the creek. I did so, and found what the leaves of summer had obscured. I walked under the overhanging rock and sat in that seat, which was exactly as they had described it, in the wilderness at last. *Off the trail*, as Gary Snyder would say—where true discovery lies.

> *Before long, we were far from the lake, far from any trail, in a world of fallen trees, mounds of bear droppings, and unmapped gorges.*

■ ■ ■

IV

I spent the summer of 2011 rushing through the Gorge. It wasn't until October, when the Gorge was in the full flush of autumn colors and perfect weather that I began to slow down. I had invited my brother Michael to help map several long trails: the Sheltowee Trace, the Rough Trail, and the Swift Camp Creek Trail. He stands in marked contrast to me; an Eagle Scout, Michael studied the wilderness from community college in the Adirondacks through his undergraduate work at the University of Montana. Unlike me, he could survive in the forest. He knows gear, he knows plants, and he knows how to be in the woods, but also just how to enjoy it without expectation, with pure joy. It's ironic that I often chide him for not having read *Walden*.

I told him how busy I had been with these trails, and he told me flatly that I had to relax and just enjoy where I was. On each hike we did, I tried to see the place through his eyes. We strolled down the trails at a leisurely pace, stopping to explore rock shelters, identify paw-paws, or examine enormous fisher spiders. Even though I was photographing and mapping, I gave more consideration to the wind in the trees, the light on limestone, the meditative music of Gladie Creek.

Just paying attention to a landscape will reveal what Wendell Berry has called "marks," the evidences of human use. The Gorge is rife with marks: splash dams, old road grades, even a settlement. I had read Ellesa Clay High's *Past Titan Rock*, a human history of the Red River Gorge, or at least of its late-nineteenth and early-twentieth century settlers. It amazes me the transformations the Gorge has gone through in terms of its economies. People have found many things to extract. Sometimes they have done this thoughtfully, but more often they have not. Farming has been attempted and was mildly successful in the lowlands along the river, but it was devastating on the steep slopes above the banks. Long before the roads, railroads were punched through the forest, the timber hauled out. After the wood was gone and the Forest Service took over, the land was managed for fire suppression, and this has resulted in the second-growth forest growing back at an astonishing rate. But it has also led to the near-disappearance of wild blueberries, which thrive on fire. Now it is managed for recreation.

In a sense, I have also managed the Gorge for my own ends. I have used it to extract an experience, a book contract, and continuing royalty checks. I've gotten obsessive about hiking every unmarked trail, finding every arch, naming every tree, but only recently have I read about its Native American past, about the stunning archeological finds. Once I saw a petroglyph, likely by luck. I hadn't known that bobcats were once established here, that the resurgence of black bears was more a reclamation than an anomaly. Though I can readily identify and avoid poison ivy, I have yet to see the yellow lady slipper orchids that grow in the Gorge.

Nevertheless, I have clearly fallen in love with the Red River Gorge. I know that now, but I still have to think on it, to try to see this place from various perspectives. All those that came before me—what did they see that I've missed? But I suspect this is not solely a matter of seeing, but of *feeling*. My brother has spent so much time in the mountains, in the wilderness, that he's forged a relationship with it that has nothing to do with money, or time, or anything else but appreciation. Compared to him, I sometimes feel like a visitor to the woods. A tourist.

Once, on a late autumn walk along the Rough Trail, I felt myself wanting to be someone else. Much of that trail I'd hiked on other loops, on other mapping expeditions, and so I was familiar with many of its sights: Signature Rock, Chimney Top Creek. But soon I passed even these familiar places and headed onto a stretch of trail I'd not been on, a new territory. I was determined to extract nothing, to approach the forest not in the mindset of a lumberman, or a miner, or a vacationer—or, rather, in what I imagined such a mindset to be. I did not want to cull an experience, or even to create one, but rather just to *be* in the forest. To be truly with myself, the way Muir and Thoreau learned to be, the way my brother learned, too.

The final stretch of trail proved quiet, solicitous of the peculiar solitude I could only really achieve in the mountains. Once I passed the last backpacker camp, I saw no one. I heard only the call of pileated woodpeckers in the trees, the clatter of limbs. I stopped to watch a flurry of leaf-fall, as a light wind shook the trees and filled the air with gold. I left the camera in

Once I passed the last backpacker camp, I saw no one. I heard only the call of pileated woodpeckers in the trees, the clatter of limbs.

its case, and kept my eyes and ears fixed on what was before me. I had enough photos for my book. It was the feeling I wanted, and I found it there, rising in me.

I carried this feeling up from the final hollow, from the thread of Parched Corn Creek and the dusty rock shelters. It was the feeling that, for a few hours, I was free, not because I was free of the usual humdrum, day-to-day existence, which we're never really free of, but rather because I realized the daily life for what it was: a passing cloud, a shower of leaves coming to rest on the ground. I had only to let go of my expectations and the idea that the forest, indeed the world, owed me something for my trouble.

A Forest Service employee I once met thought all signs should be removed from wilderness areas. I objected that people would get lost. *That's the point,* he suggested. *It's wilderness.* More and more I've come to believe this. To get at the true sense of wilderness—and for some, this is the whole point of exploration—one must learn orienteering. One must bushwhack. As uncomfortable as that sounds, it is the comfort that must be thwarted to enter the mystery of wilderness. A guidebook is a doorway, a place to begin, but in the end we must leave it home. I have discovered that loving a landscape—or a person or a home—means to simply pay attention to it, to be as richly conscious of it as is possible. By loving a landscape, we become a part of it.

Some things, wrote Barry Lopez, must remain a mystery, and wilderness is one of them. Despite a congressional designation, a Wilderness Area is anything but; following the six-foot wide tread of the Pacific Coast Trail towards Diamond Peak, we only *think* we're entering wilderness, though in fact that trail is maintained not just by the Forest Service, but by abundant footfall. Those who actually leave the trail are few, and even the campsites tend to be established. The whole purpose of through-hiking the PCT, start-to-finish, threatens to become the ultimate Point A to Point B experience unless we are vigilant. It may be that most through-hikers shy away from entering the true wilderness; indeed, most people would be afraid to. What would happen to Yosemite if, as Ed Abbey suggested, we actually removed the roads and, hence, the easy access? What if this were to happen in the Red River Gorge?

On a perfect day in October, ambling along the Rough Trail, I came down to a small confluence of creeks in a hollow, nearly paradisiacal in its beauty. I lingered. I listened. Finally, I sat down next to a tiny waterfall and watched the light flash over the lip of exposed limestone. A yellow leaf fell, a monarch butterfly drifted, and I wondered that for a moment I could not tell them apart. ■

HALFWAY BETWEEN NYC AND MIAMI

Rivendell

Now that summer days enlarge
under the green screen doors,
what if to-morrow
borrows a month, a year?
A longer breath off the bluff.
I would sit that morrow
on seven lines of poetry:

I was not born or raised here
still, I know—wind and soft rain
begin the same, its bustle
sent silently in heaves out
among the trees—and the pang
for either blows in from
that same barren place.

CATHERINE MOORE

BOOK REVIEW

Laura Long & Doug Van Gundy, Eds. *Eyes Glowing at the Edge of the Woods: Fiction and Poetry from West Virginia.* Morgantown, W.Va.: Vandalia Books, 2017. 368 pages. Softcover. $32.99.

Reviewed by Emily Masters

Eyes Glowing at the Edge of the Woods: Fiction and Poetry from West Virginia is a collection of short stories and poems from some of West Virginia's best writers and poets. Edited by Laura Long and Doug Van Gundy, the anthology is an important contribution to Appalachian literature and provides a beautiful showcase of some of West Virginia's limitless writing talent by featuring short stories and poetry from sixty-three writers and poets from all different walks of life but who share in common a connection to the Mountain State. In this collection, Long and Van Gundy, both

writers themselves, have fashioned "a mosaic crafted from many voices, united by this place, and the quality of the work" that avoids stereotypical representations of the Appalachian experience.

The anthology takes its title from a line in Irene McKinney's poem "Handholds," and as a further tribute to this beloved West Virginia poet, her poem "To My Reader" introduces the collection. Well-known writers and poets including Denise Giardina, Marc Harshman, Ann Pancake, and Jayne Anne Phillips are featured in the collection, and their writing is certainly a treat to any readers who are interested in high quality Appalachian writing. The editors have struck a good balance between short stories and poems, so readers will not find themselves bogged down by one or the other, with the flow of the pieces carrying the reader effortlessly through the anthology.

Eyes Glowing at the Edge of the Woods proves to readers that West Virginian writers are inspired not only by the world outside their windows but also by current global and social issues. Stories and poems ranging from the front porch to as far away as Greece (in the case of Gail Galloway Adams' "Olives") reminds readers that Appalachia is more far reaching than many stereotypes allow. Themes of sexuality, environmental issues (as in Matthew Neill Null's "Natural Resources,"), and class issues are found throughout the poems and short stories and firmly root the anthology in the modern world, showing that West Virginia and Appalachia as a whole are perhaps not as old-fashioned and traditional as many who live outside the region believe. In "A History of Barbed Wire," Jeff Mann's narrator confronts the difficulties of being gay in a small town with startling clarity: "The mountain men have always frightened me, but now I realize that I also desire them, though I know my lust, if expressed, would be met only with contempt and violence." Null's short story "Natural Resources" examines the ways in which overhunting can have detrimental effects ecologically. In selecting such pieces, the editors achieve a balance in the poems and short stories between an appreciation of West Virginia and a healthy questioning of some of its more conservative traditions.

Perfect for readers who want to take a journey to West Virginia, the anthology provides something relatable for everyone. Readers should expect an emotional journey, one in which they will find themselves heartbroken and on the verge of tears, and alternately laughing at some of the more light-hearted writing.

In the goal of creating a mosaic of writing, Long and Van Gundy succeed because each writer and poet's representation of West Virginia is distinct and reveals a diverse depiction of the state. Readers of the anthology might just look up to see friendly animal eyes glowing at the edge of their own woods. ■

CONTRIBUTORS

Deborah Reed Downing is a Kentucky native currently living in New Orleans where she serves on the English faculty of Delgado Community College. Her coming of age novel, *Not Stopping at Mammoth Cave*, nears completion.

Robert Gipe is the author of *Trampoline*, winner of the 2016 Weatherford Award in Fiction. He lives in Harlan, Kentucky, and grew up in Kingsport, Tennessee. His fiction has appeared in *Appalachian Heritage, Still, Motif,* and *Pine Mountain Sand & Gravel.*

Emily Hancock lives in the Blue Ridge Mountains of Virginia and works as a letterpress printer and hand-bookbinder. She has received awards for her poetry from the Poetry Council of North Carolina and the Oxford Guild of Printers (England), and has been published in the *Greensboro Review, Appalachian Journal,* and *Grey Sparrow Journal.*

Jeffrey Helton is a native of Western North Carolina and an alumnus of Berea College, where he studied English and Philosophy. He is the founder and former editor of *Pollen*, an online literary magazine dedicated to the relationship between folks and food in Appalachia. Helton spends his free writing in most genres under the sun. His work has been featured in *Still: The Journal* and *Limestone.*

Sean Patrick Hill is a poet and writer in Louisville, Kentucky. He is a recipient of an Al Smith Fellowship from the Kentucky Arts Council and of grants and fellowships from the Vermont Studio Center and the Elizabeth George Foundation. He is the author of three collections of poems, most recently *Hibernaculum*. His work has appeared in *Kentucky Monthly, LEO Weekly,* and in many other journals.

Silas House is the nationally bestselling author of six novels, most recently *Same Sun Here* (with Neela Vaswani), as well as three plays and one book of creative nonfiction. He is a frequent contributor to the *New York Times* and serves as the NEH Chair of Appalachian Studies at Berea College and on the fiction faculty at Spalding University's MFA in creative writing. His novel *Southernmost* will be published in June 2018.

Since earning a degree in English from Marietta College in 1993, **Jimmy Long** has pursued a career in the financial services industry. He has recently resumed an active writing life in Charleston, West Virginia, where he works and lives with his family of five. In 2016, Long won first place in poetry for his submission to *Mountain Ink Literary Journal.*

Maurice Manning's most recent poetry collections are *One Man's Dark* and *The Gone and the Going Away.* A former Guggenheim fellow, Manning has been a finalist for the Pulitzer Prize and is a member of The Fellowship of Southern Writers. He teaches at Transylvania University and in the MFA Program for Writers at Warren Wilson College.

Emily Masters is a senior English major at Berea College where she works as a teaching assistant for Silas House and as a student editor for *Appalachian Heritage* and *Apollon* e-journal. She is from Monteagle, Tennessee, where she lives on a farm with her family. Her work has recently been published in *The Pikeville Review.*

Catherine Moore is the author of *Story, 921b Elysian Fields Avenue - Return to Sender,* and *Wetlands.* Her poetry appears in *Southampton Review, Cider Press Review, Wicked Alice, Blue Fifth Review, Caesura, Still: the Journal* and in various anthologies. A Walker Percy fellow, she won the 2014 Gearhart Poetry Prize. Moore earned a Master of Fine Arts from the University of Tampa, and she teaches at a community college. She's tweetable @CatPoetic.

One of **Charlotte Morgan**'s stories is included in the Pushcart Prize Collections. She holds an MFA from Virginia Commonwealth University where she studied with Lee Smith and Paule Marshall. Her first novel, *One August Day,* was considered for the annual Fiction Prize by the Library of Virginia. For twenty-five years she has been writer-in-residence at Nimrod Hall Summer Arts Program.

Born in West Virginia, **Br. Paul Quenon**, OCSO entered the Trappists in 1958 at the Abbey of Gethsemani in Kentucky, where Thomas Merton was his Novice Master. He has been publishing poems and photographs for the last twenty years. Quenon's latest books of poetry are *Unquiet Vigil* and *Bells of the Hours.*

Jacob Strautmann's poems have appeared in *The Harlequin, Salamander Magazine, The Boston Globe, Agni Online, The Appalachian Journal, Solstice, Jam Tarts,* and *Quiddity* (from which he won the Editor's Prize in Poetry). He is a contributing editor for *Salamander Magazine.* He holds an MA from Boston University, where he teaches creative writing and is the Managing Director of Boston Playwrights' Theatre.

Allison Thorpe is a writer from Lexington, Kentucky. Her recent work has appeared or is forthcoming in *Pine Mountain Sand and Gravel, Green Hills Literary Lantern, Roanoke Review, Split Rock Review, Pembroke Magazine, Hamilton Stone Review,* and *Pleiades.*

Jessie van Eerden is the author of two novels, *Glorybound* and *My Radio Radio.* Her work has appeared in *Oxford American, Image, Cimarron Review, The River Teeth Reader,* and *Best American Spiritual Writing,* among other places. Van Eerden received an MFA in nonfiction from the University of Iowa in 2007. She currently directs the low-residency MFA program at West Virginia Wesleyan College.

Marianne Worthington is co-founder and poetry editor of *Still: The Journal,* an online literary magazine. Her work has appeared or is forthcoming in *Oxford American, CALYX, Grist, Shenandoah, The Louisville Review, Southern Poetry Anthology,* and *Vinegar and Char: Southern Food in Verse.* She lives, writes, and teaches in southeast Kentucky.

UNITED STATES POSTAL SERVICE ®

Statement of Ownership, Management, and Circulation (All Periodicals Publications Except Requester Publications)

1. Publication Title	2. Publication Number	3. Filing Date
Appalachian Heritage	0 3 6 3 - 2 8 1 8	September 28, 2017
4. Issue Frequency	5. Number of Issues Published Annually	6. Annual Subscription Price
quarterly (Winter, Spring, Summer, Fall)	4 (3 this year)	$30 individuals $60 institutions

7. Complete Mailing Address of Known Office of Publication (Not printer) (Street, city, county, state, and ZIP+4®)

The Loyal Jones Appalachian Center, CPO Box 2166, Berea College, Madison County, Berea, KY 40404

Contact Person: Suzi Waters

Telephone (Include area code): 919-962-4201

8. Complete Mailing Address of Headquarters or General Business Office of Publisher (Not printer)

The University of North Carolina Press, 116 South Boundary St, Chapel Hill, Orange County, NC 27514

9. Full Names and Complete Mailing Addresses of Publisher, Editor, and Managing Editor (Do not leave blank)

Publisher (Name and complete mailing address)

The University of North Carolina Press, 116 South Boundary St, Chapel Hill, Orange County, NC 27514

Editor (Name and complete mailing address)

Jason K. Howard, The Loyal Jones Appalachian Center, CPO Box 2166, Berea College Madison County, Berea KY 40404

Managing Editor (Name and complete mailing address)

same as Editor above

10. Owner (Do not leave blank. If the publication is owned by a corporation, give the name and address of the corporation immediately followed by the names and addresses of all stockholders owning or holding 1 percent or more of the total amount of stock. If not owned by a corporation, give the names and addresses of the individual owners. If owned by a partnership or other unincorporated firm, give its name and address as well as those of each individual owner. If the publication is published by a nonprofit organization, give its name and address.)

Full Name	Complete Mailing Address
The Loyal Jones Appalachian Center	CPO Box 2166, 205 North Main St, Berea KY 40404

11. Known Bondholders, Mortgagees, and Other Security Holders Owning or Holding 1 Percent or More of Total Amount of Bonds, Mortgages, or Other Securities. If none, check box → ☐ None

Full Name	Complete Mailing Address

12. Tax Status (For completion by nonprofit organizations authorized to mail at nonprofit rates) (Check one)

The purpose, function, and nonprofit status of this organization and the exempt status for federal income tax purposes:

XX Has Not Changed During Preceding 12 Months

☐ Has Changed During Preceding 12 Months (Publisher must submit explanation of change with this statement)

PS Form 3526, July 2014 (Page 1 of 4 (see instructions page 4)) PSN: 7530-01-000-9931 PRIVACY NOTICE: See our privacy policy on www.usps.com

13. Publication Title	14. Issue Date for Circulation Data Below	
Appalachian Heritage	Spring 2017, 45#2 June 14,2017	
15. Extent and Nature of Circulation	**Average No. Copies Each Issue During Preceding 12 Months**	**No. Copies of Single Issue Published Nearest to Filing Date**
a. Total Number of Copies *(Net press run)*	800	800
b. Paid Circulation *(By Mail and Outside the Mail)* (1) Mailed Outside-County Paid Subscriptions Stated on PS Form 3541 (Include paid distribution above nominal rate, advertiser's proof copies, and exchange copies)	335	323
(2) Mailed In-County Paid Subscriptions Stated on PS Form 3541 *(Include paid distribution above nominal rate, advertiser's proof copies, and exchange copies)*		
(3) Paid Distribution Outside the Mails Including Sales Through Dealers and Carriers, Street Vendors, Counter Sales, and Other Paid Distribution Outside USPS®		
(4) Paid Distribution by Other Classes of Mail Through the USPS (e.g., First-Class Mail®)		
c. Total Paid Distribution *(Sum of 15b (1), (2), (3), and (4))*	335	323
d. Free or Nominal Rate Distribution *(By Mail and Outside the Mail)* (1) Free or Nominal Rate Outside-County Copies included on PS Form 3541	61	75
(2) Free or Nominal Rate In-County Copies Included on PS Form 3541		
(3) Free or Nominal Rate Copies Mailed at Other Classes Through the USPS (e.g., First-Class Mail)		
(4) Free or Nominal Rate Distribution Outside the Mail *(Carriers or other means)*		
e. Total Free or Nominal Rate Distribution *(Sum of 15d (1), (2), (3) and (4))*	61	75
f. Total Distribution *(Sum of 15c and 15e)*	396	398
g. Copies not Distributed *(See Instructions to Publishers #4 (page #3))*	404	402
h. Total *(Sum of 15f and g)*	800	800
i. Percent Paid *(15c divided by 15f times 100)*	85%	81%

* If you are claiming electronic copies, go to line 16 on page 3. If you are not claiming electronic copies, skip to line 17 on page 3.

17. Publication of Statement of Ownership

XX If the publication is a general publication, publication of this statement is required. Will be printed in the Fall 2017 issue of this publication.

☐ Publication not required.

18. Signature and Title of Editor, Publisher, Business Manager, or Owner

Robert Dirks[illegible]
CFO, UNC PRESS

Date 9/28/2017

I certify that all information furnished on this form is true and complete. I understand that anyone who furnishes false or misleading information on this form or who omits material or information requested on the form may be subject to criminal sanctions (including fines and imprisonment) and/or civil sanctions (including civil penalties).

PS Form 3526, July 2014